This book makes you feel better, by thinking better. This book makes you feel good, by thinking good.

Some of the wisest questions I've ever heard were: 'How should I pray? What should I think about? How can I improve my thoughts and thus my emotions and ultimately my actions?' Those questions are answered in this book. Sagaciously and with an entertaining and upbeat transparency that is rare in modern writing.

I think differently and more positively because of the affirmations and thoughts I've been exhorted to meditate upon in this book. You can't help but feel better after reading Jean's thoughts on thought.

If you want more control over your life and emotions, this book will show you how, if you want more understanding over why things happen, this book shows you where to look, if you want to find answers, this book shows you where to look without giving away the surprise ending."

Mark Faust, Principal

Faust@EchelonManagement.com
www.EchelonManagement.com
Growing business since 1990.
8044 Montgomery Road, #260
Cincinnati, Ohio 45236

Growth or Bust! #1 best selling business book at Barnes & Noble SW Ohio. Also available at Hudson's.

"Jean Costa, where were you when I was younger? Your vision and powerful insights – underscored by your uncommon gifting in shaping ideas and creating texture – jump off the page."

Reader – and this is not an overstatement – your life can be changed, for how we live begins with what we intend. In *Creating Positive Affirmations, Living an Intentional Life*, Jean puts it this way: "An intention is a phrase stated in the present tense about something which you want to bring into reality." By the way, Jean is in cahoots with a biblical writer who said, as we think in our heart, so are we.

Slowly read; ingesting her ideas as they move you from now to where you want to be. Underline. Re-read. Tell another. Chat with a friend about what caught your attention. This is life, and it is good. I know dozens I'll send this to.

Brian C Stiller

Global Ambassador – The World Evangelical Alliance
President Emeritus – Tyndale University College & Seminary

CREATING POSITIVE AFFIRMATIONS, LIVING AN INTENTIONAL LIFE

A compilation of affirmations and stories designed to nurture and empower.

JEAN A. COSTA

The profits from the sale of this book supports the Duke Cancer Patient Support Program's Pink Ribbon Yoga Retreat. The annual retreat, founded in 2005, was formed to bring together women fighting breast cancer--from those who are newly diagnosed to women who have been thriving for decades. Through a shared yoga journey women from all over the country find support, camaraderie, healing, joy and peace. To remove financial barriers that could prevent participation, this four-day retreat is offered at a low cost and provides scholarships for those who need additional support.

© 2014 Jean A. Costa.
All rights reserved.

No part of this book may be reproduced, stored in a retrieval system, or transmitted by any means without the written permission of the author.

Affirmation Press

ISBN 9781944662

Printed in the United States of America

Contents

Introduction xi

Welcome xiii

    Beginning the Journey xiv

    Avoid Negatives xv

    Emotions xvi

    How To Use This Book xviii

Spring 1

    The Path to Health, Forgiveness 1

    Rising with Christ 5

    Blessings and Friends 8

    Imaginary Conversations 12

    The Fabulous Female 16

    You Only Live Once 19

    Keeping Out of the Cave of Phantoms 23

    May All Your Dreams Come True 26

    Claiming Your Power 29

    Fun! 34

    Hope is a Choice 36

    Gratitude and Forgiveness 39

    The Power of Prayer 42

Summer 45
   Dancing for Life 45
   Who Are These People? 49
   Who Would You Die For? 53
   An Unexpected Life 56
   Perception 59
   The Big Picture 62
   Faith or Fear? You Choose 65
   Loving Speech 69
   The Third Klesha, Attachment 72
   Younger Next Year 75
   Answered Prayer 79
   Learning to Love Your Life 82
   Financial Prosperity 85

Fall 88
   Letting Go of Childhood Limitations 88
   An Ethical Will 91
   And Then the Wind Chime Rang 94
   Outward Bounds 97
   Passionate for Freedom 100
   Giving up the Struggle 103
   Love and Grief 106
   Worry and Anxiety 109

Put Your Glasses On, Change Your Vision 112

Easy to Unhook 116

Miraculous Happenings... 120

Time is My Friend 124

Healthy Mind, Healthy Body 127

Winter 130

How to Get Ready for the End Times................................. 130

You Can Change the World.. 134

Field of Dreams 137

Perfecting Christmas 140

A Year-End Review, Looking Back Before You Go Forward 142

Manifesting the New Year 145

Finding Your Joy 148

Embracing Adventure 152

Nurturing Relationships 156

Living a Compassionate Life.. 159

Not If When... 163

Love Is Your Only Job... 166

The Fragile Ego 170

Epilogue 173
Acknowledgements 175

Dedicated to my husband, Sandy Costa, the love of my life.

Introduction

When I first met Jean Costa, I realized that there was something very special about her. Jean has an aura of gentleness, of compassion, of positivity that immediately made me relax. As we talked, I could feel my soul stir as if we had been lifelong friends. I immediately trusted her and felt I could tell her anything.

There are dozens of really good reasons to read this book. Actually, we all should read it several times. For me, one of the core reasons is to recalibrate in my brain the meaning of the word "intention" in my life.

The common definition of the word "intention" is "An aim or plan." However, the first thought most people have when they see the word "intention" is not a positive one. With all the crime shows on TV there is usually a subplot around the "intent" of the criminal; whether the crime was "premeditated" or not.

And then there is the whole "The road to Hell is paved..." thing.

This wonderful book by my good friend Jean Costa has forever changed the meaning of "intention" for me.

The second definition of the word is from the world of medicine. It says that "intention" is "The healing process of a wound."

Therein lies the beauty of Jean's words.

In a world constantly pounding and cutting us with guilt, unattainable expectations and self-fulfilling disappointments, Jean's melodious words provide a song to our souls. Through intention, we can heal ourselves of these wounds the world wants to inflict upon us and instead soar with gratitude and possibility.

As you read this book, imagine yourself relaxing on a porch on a beautiful spring afternoon, drinking a refreshing cup of coffee or cool glass of tea as the soft breeze occasionally brings you the sweet scents of the season from the flower garden and honeysuckle vines. Imagine Jean is sitting with you, her eyes dancing as she tells you these stories and how intentionality and gratitude can transform your life.

The word "intention" comes from the Latin word "intentionem" which means "a stretching out." Open your heart and let this beautiful book help you stretch the positivity in your life.

Oie Osterkamp
Executive Director
Ronald McDonald House of Durham
506 Alexander Avenue
Durham, NC 27705
919-286-9305 office
919-210-0600 mobile
http://www.ronaldhousedurham.org/

Welcome

The saying, "We cannot control the wind but we can decide how to set the sail," is the essence of this book. *Creating Positive Affirmations* is about living an intentional life. It's about the power of making conscious choices about how you want to live life, what you want to change, what you want to improve upon, and what you value and want to fully appreciate. It's about being intentional, mindful about what you are thinking, especially about those things you say to yourself. The wind may blow you all over the world and take you to places you do or do not choose but it is your attitude during the journey and when you arrive that will determine every aspect of the adventure and you can determine that mindset by carefully choosing your self-talk.

Our greatest human ability is the ability to control what and how we think. This book is about using that ability to enhance your life. When I began writing out my affirmations, I discovered the power of controlling my thoughts. Once I took charge of what I was thinking, I took charge of my life. I also found joy and power in the process of creating the affirmations. I love testing the words, seeing what resonates and deciding what is so important to me that I would want to focus on it day after day. One of the most interesting aspects of creating affirmations is when I find I am faced with a situation with which I have consistently struggled and I find myself responding differently than before, with more understanding, dignity, and grace. This is the ultimate gift of living an intentional life.

Beginning the Journey

I have journaled since I was a young girl. I used to take strips of paper and staple them together and use that for my diary. Then I was given a fancy diary with a lock and key. I loved it! That was the beginning, and for over twenty years, I've written daily in the style of Julia Cameron's *The Artist's Way*. I have all sorts of journals: I have travel journals; I have a journal chronicling my journeys through graduate school and breast cancer; I have a beautiful leather journal I used when I studied yoga at Kripalu. My daily journals are usually spiral bound 6" x 9" notebooks. I also have a favorite type of pen and I always write first thing in the morning. It's meditative; it's healing; it's nurturing; and it's empowering. It's a practice that has guided me and given me clarity when I felt lost and confused. I start every entry with a prayer and I end with prayer and hope that everything in between is guided by spirit. My journal holds all my affirmations. It's where they are born and grow and become reality. Certainly, one doesn't need to journal daily to create affirmations but for me it's all part of the joy of creation.

One of the first steps to creating an affirmation is to take a look at your "self-talk." Notice those things you say to yourself throughout your day. Sometimes you're having the conversation when you're alone; sometimes you're not. What are the phrases you've adopted over the years? Are they empowering or demeaning? This book is about changing the negative things you tell yourself. You can do it! Anyone can do it. Why would you want to start saying positive things to yourself or about yourself? Will it make any difference? Yes, it will.

What exactly is an affirmation? What does it look like? How should it sound? What phrases work? Which ones do not? An affirmation is a statement that affirms (and makes firm) that which you believe. You can have positive or negative affirmations. Most of us have lived our lives telling ourselves about our faults. We also rarely hesitate to tell others about our faults. For example, someone may compliment your outfit. What is your normal response? Or perhaps they tell you what a wonderful job you did on a project. What do you say when that happens? Can you imagine saying, "Thank you. I did do a great job, didn't I?" You don't have to say it out loud, but perhaps you could start saying it to yourself and you don't need to wait for someone to compliment you. You can begin saying it right now, "I really do a great job."

Avoid Negatives

When creating an affirmation avoid the word "not" it won't work to your benefit, and it may even work to your detriment. There are some phrases you can use instead of enlisting the negative. For example, "I release or I let go of." Two of my affirmations using those phrases are, "I let go of fear and anxiety," and "I release myself from my childhood limitations." It's simply more effective than saying, "I will not let fear and anxiety influence my life." Can you hear the difference? Can you feel the difference? What are some things in your life you'd like to let go of or release?

I heard a story many years ago about a mother teaching her daughter to drive. There was a huge boulder in the road ahead. The mother kept reminding her daughter about it. "Don't go near the boulder," and "Don't hit the boulder." What do you think happened? They were both so focused on missing the rock in the road that they drove right into it. The same thing can happen if you include negatives in your affirmation. You won't hear the "not" and you'll move right into the place you're trying to avoid.

Sometimes it's helpful to write out an affirmation without too much thought and then take time to fine-tune it. Begin by taking a few minutes and re-reading the words. You are looking for words that stir an emotion in you. Don't over analyze. Let the sentence be a statement of how you want to perceive your life. Write it in the present tense. It may be a statement you have a difficult time believing, but try it anyway. Sometimes those affirmations are the most powerful. I have a dear friend whose affirmation is, "I am a gifted and talented artist." When she first claimed that, she did not feel that way—but that's how she wanted to feel. It worked! She faked it until she made it. She now feels like the gifted and talented artist she is. Her affirmation led her to the steps that led her to believe in herself and to expand her gifts and talents.

Emotions

It is helpful to use words that resonate deeply within you. Try out some of the words; see if they cause a visceral reaction. One of my affirmations is related to the concept of "staying connected to the Divine." I believe that we are spirit having a human experience and that with awareness and quiet we can connect to God's Divine Grace. You can define that any way you like. I believe it's available to us and can lead us to a peace beyond that of human comprehension. So I created the affirmation: "When I pray and meditate, I enter into union with the Divine; miracles are created and without struggle manifest themselves." I love the words divine, miracles, without struggle and manifest. When I hear them I think, "hope." I have found that I now spend more time in prayer, more time in silence. Miracles? Oh, yes, they have manifested. Is it because I am paying more attention, waiting for them to appear or is it because they have multiplied because of my time spent with Spirit? Do I really care why? Would you?

An example of how an affirmation worked for me in my life was when I went for my first training session with a young man at a local gym. He seemed to be in quite a hurry. He called me "sweetie" and at the end of a half hour he indicated that we were done. That was all I got for "free" because he "needed to make a living." I didn't expect the session to be free. I actually thought I was buying an hour of time to fine-tune my workout. When he walked away I couldn't tell you what I was feeling, but I knew what had just taken place didn't feel good. I waited a short while and noticed it was my inclination to just let the whole episode go.

Why would I do that? Because my self-talk over the years had persuaded me to avoid conflict. I have also told myself that I am not an assertive person. There have been many incidents when I felt almost abused but I didn't fully recognize them at the moment and I didn't feel empowered enough to stand up for myself. Two of my affirmations are, "I stand in my power," and "I am worthy, I am valuable, I am lovable." So, this time, instead of listening to my negative self-talk, I recognized that I had been badly treated and spoke to the young man at the gym. We resolved the issue (which revolved around some miscommunication) and he won't be calling me "sweetie" any longer.

Not sure it will work for you? Think about this: All those negative statements you've been telling yourself for as long as you can remember: How have they been working? They've probably worked quite well but unfortunately not to your benefit. Changing them to positive statements will work too and think how much better you'll feel.

One example of an affirmation I use in my daily practice is, "When I stay focused on the present, I am calmer and more peaceful." I created this one because I believe what is truly important is today. Worry magnifies my difficulties and diminishes my ability to live fully in the present moment. Anxieties almost always arise when I fail to put all my effort into the here and now. I am calmer and more peaceful when I focus more on the gifts of each day, instead of worrying about tomorrow or reliving something unpleasant from the past.

The quality of my life is all about how I perceive every event and person, including myself. If I can change myself for the better won't that help others? If you did the same thing wouldn't that help both you and the world (or at least your world)? It's an amazing process. Take full advantage of it. Write your affirmations down every day, post them on your bathroom mirror, by your doorway, on your computer … and then wait! You will have created a set of affirmations and taken the necessary steps to change your life in ways you never before dreamed possible.

How To Use This Book

Creating Positive Affirmations is divided into the four seasons. The affirmations are some of my personal affirmations. Each one is followed by a story.

The intentions I share here are only to serve as an example. They may or may not resonate with you. Your life's focus may be very different from mine. Feel free to use any that do work for you, but please take the time to write out your life's dreams and priorities, to intentionally design your life, and then to create your own personal affirmations.

As you can well imagine, there is a huge amount of information available on the Internet about affirmations. Once you begin the journey, inspiration will come from places you never even imagined. I believe God wants us to live full, rich lives. He/She does not want us to just drift along. We were created with minds and free wills so we could choose those things that best serve God and our brothers and sisters. By taking charge of our thoughts and therefore our behaviors, we are honoring God and bringing a richness to our lives and to all those whose lives we touch that would not occur if we did not make the effort to live an intentional life.

Spring

The Path to Health, Forgiveness

Affirmation: *I freely forgive myself and others.*

What does it mean to forgive someone? What does forgiveness look like? Does it mean you must now become the offender's friend? Does it mean you must forget whatever happened that unsettled you or brought you pain? Is forgiveness an emotion, or a conscious decision? Once you make that decision, are you finished, or is it a process?

Have you ever had something happen in your life that you could not let go of? Something that seemed to haunt you? Something that you were sure you had "gotten over" that kept appearing? Something that kept coming up even in your dreams?

Forgiveness is a topic that appears in all spiritual teachings and in many writings about improving one's physical health. Of course, one can't really separate the two. Forgiveness requires letting go of resentment and hurt. It offers one the opportunity to let go of perceived—or actual—injuries and move forward. It does not demand that you dismiss someone's poor behavior or that you and your offender need to continue a relationship. It is not an emotion; it is a conscious decision and it can take a lot of work!

I can be fascinated by my own reaction to what I think is a "done deal." I'm sure I've put that issue behind me. I've prayed about it, I've journaled about it, and I've made a conscious decision to not hold onto whatever it is that has caused me pain, whether or not it was intentional. "I'm good with that," I tell myself. And then something happens. There's some recollection of the event and whoosh, I feel like I'm starting all over again, but if I've worked on it, I'm probably starting a little further up the spiral than in the beginning.

The Buddhists say when you don't forgive someone it's like holding a hot coal in your hand and expecting it to burn the other person. Christ's main message was about love and forgiveness. Even after he had been tortured and humiliated, He asked his Father to forgive His persecutors: "Father, forgive them for they know not what they do." (Luke 23:34) The one prayer he taught us, The Lord's Prayer, says, "Forgive us our trespasses as we forgive those who trespass against us." At one of the church studies in which I was a participant, the main topic was forgiveness. It was presented as a tool to bring one closer to God. A yoga workshop I also attended, taught in the tradition of Thich Nhat Hanh, had a primary focus on forgiveness. The Mayo Clinic has a whole website devoted to how forgiveness promotes health and healing[1]. There's also a healing movement that encourages people who have lost loved ones to violent crimes to connect with the criminal and to offer an olive branch. I cannot even imagine the fortitude and stamina that such a process must take but there are those amazing people out there who accomplish such a monumental feat.

My book group read *The Girl in the Blue Dress*, a fictional story of the wife of Charles Dickens by Gaynor Arnold Catherine Taylor. It created a great deal of conversation (which is one reason I am part of a book group). In the story a woman goes about healing herself of every shred of animosity she had with regard to those who had mistreated her and she was very poorly treated, some would say even abused. Her husband disowned her making her leave her home and six of her eight living children. Her sister took over the household and kept the family from contacting her. Her husband had what everyone thought was a mistress. Even after her children were grown, they did not connect with her. She had a lot about which to be angry. She had a lot of justified reasons for resentment and she had quite a bit, as you can well imagine. But, after

---

[1] www.mayoclinic.com/health/forgiveness

her husband died, she openly accepted those people in her family who wanted to make restitution. She didn't demand a thing from them other than an open mind and heart. She approached her husband's rumored mistress and even made peace with her.

What do you think? Was she a weak, desperate person, or was she wise and strong? Was she so accustomed to being used as a doormat that she no longer knew how to stand up for herself, or was she so relieved to let go of years of loneliness and shunning? All I know is that I found inspiration in her actions to make peace with her pain. It's so easy to cling to resentments, to work them over in our minds until we know we are right and our nemesis is oh-so-very wrong and perhaps even evil. But, truly, when I do that those emotions, those conversations I have with myself don't disturb that other person in any way. The only one who is unsettled and disturbed is me.

One of my daily readings comes from a book called *Spiritual Insights for Daily Living*.[2] I've discovered that some things have longer "tails" than others. They can be draining and unsettling. Sometimes, I can't even imagine why these thoughts that keep coming up, have become so insistent, so obsessive. The reading from January 21 helped me with this issue: "I am now ready for a cleansing—getting rid of debris that I have harbored much too long. Anyone who at any time may have contributed to causing disharmony within me, I bring into consciousness and I see them clearly and honestly. As I visualize them, I say with feeling and complete sincerity: 'I fully and freely forgive you.'"

We are called to forgive "seventy times seven" (Matthew 18:22). One of my studies called the injuries we carry with us "wounds of the heart." We were encouraged to carefully look back on our lives and make note of every wound that had been inflicted upon us. Certainly, I've been very lucky and didn't see any reason to pursue this line of healing but, I would participate simply because I was part of the group and this was our assignment. Once I cracked open the box that held all those wounds, I was stunned to see just how many were still in there. I had things hiding

---

[2] Elizabeth Fenske, editor. 1986.

in that box I hadn't thought of in years! Once the list began, I actually found some pleasure in making it. Not only were old acquaintances on that list, but my church was there and once in a while God's name came up. Then, too, I found way down in the bottom my own name with so many things for which I had not yet forgiven myself.

Wounds of the heart take up space that can be used for love and for compassion. But what to do with them? Now that I could see them clearly, it was time to turn them over to God, an angel or two, maybe a spiritual guide. I visualized my taking the list and folding it and placing it in a new box. I closed the lid, locked the lock and placed it way up on a shelf that would take a lot of effort to reach. I am surprised when I find it has popped open on its own and I have to reseal it. There are other more tangible techniques that you may choose. One would be to actually burn the list.

Do whatever it takes to begin the healing. Yes, it takes me longer to let go of somethings than others. But, it really helps me to tell myself, ***"I freely forgive myself and others."*** I know by putting this affirmation into practice, I am happier, I am more peaceful and I am healthier. Truly, there are no justified resentments. Let them all go, especially— I repeat, especially—the ones you hold toward yourself.

Rising with Christ

Affirmation: *I know by meditating on Jesus throughout my day, I am in union with the Divine, miracles are created and without struggle my life is transformed in ways beyond my imagination.*

Lent is one of my favorite times of the year. In the Catholic tradition, ashes are smeared on one's forehead in the sign of a cross with the words, "Remember that thou art dust, and to dust thou shalt return," (Genesis 3:19). It is a reminder of our mortality and of the promises of Christ of our life to come. In the Catholic faith, Lent is the time to prepare for the death and—most importantly— the miraculous resurrection of the Son of God, Jesus Christ. Wow! What a story! We are called to travel with Him on His journey. We are called to stay present to the time, the season, the death, and the rebirth. It's a time that takes many of us out of the depths of winter and into the fullness of spring.

One of the challenges offered to us during Lent is to make it a time of sacrifice. We are encouraged to deny ourselves and to do works of mercy. We are called to do something so that we are more aware of the season of Lent during the following 46 days. It's a gift we give ourselves.

If you grew up with this concept of Lent, you know the first question most people are asked about their Lenten practice is, "What are you giving up for Lent?" While I understand it is a season of fasting and abstinence, it's also a time to rest in the Lord, to take time to listen to God's voice and to the voices of our Angels and Guides. It's a time to share those things that are truly precious to me: my time, talent, and treasure. It's a time to plant some seeds and to tend to them so they may produce the flowers and fruits of love and joy. Now, that is something that takes quite a bit of guidance. What needs to do be done to create such a bountiful harvest?

Sometime around 2003, Father Emmanuel from Africa gave the Ash Wednesday homily at my church. He had a very eastern approach to Lent. He said he had watched our American culture take on more, do more, and struggle more during Lent, and he wondered if maybe we shouldn't consider "doing less." Doing less! Oh my, now that's a self-discipline I might find very difficult to embrace. I like to "do." I like to be busy, busy, busy. I like to think I'm making a difference in the world. I'm contributing; I'm making the world a better place to live. And now, I am being challenged to do less. At another time, another visiting African priest also presented the concept of doing with less. This time he suggested we fast not only from food, but also from the Internet, television, radio, and newspapers. Instead of focusing on worldly events he suggested we use all that free time to connect with God.

How can denial and service be a gift we give ourselves? For most of us it takes an average of 40 days to develop a habit, so this type of exercise can be seen as an opportunity. I know many people who use the Lenten sacrifice as a time to diet. I can't count the number of people who have shared with me that they give up chocolate or sugar for Lent. Maybe that's worked well for them. Perhaps every time they have that craving, they find themselves more present to Christ and his sacrifice. But, besides a restrictive diet, we need to take up the badge of service, find something we can do for another. There are always so many in dire straits. How can I be of more service than I already am? Maybe I need to go through the house and give up a few coats and other items of clothing? My dear friend, Joanne Dawe, is always reminding me that someone else could be using the items I have left untouched for months (and in some cases, years). Perhaps it's a time for me to be a prayer warrior. How can I add more prayer to my daily practice, especially for those most in need? Maybe I can send a note or make a call once or twice a week to friends I haven't touched base with in a while? I can pray for them, offer up the activities of the day for them, and send them a visible sign of my love, like a note or a card, even an email might work. I'm sure you can think of many other ways to give back.

What can I give up? What new habit can I develop over the Lenten season that won't simply reduce my waistline but will add to the quality of my life and hopefully the lives of all those I touch? For this Lenten season I decided to give up ingratitude. Ingratitude is defined in the dictionary as "forgetfulness or poor return for kindness received." A synonym is "thanklessness."

I live a life full of abundant blessings. I am a very lucky woman. I am loved by my family and have many wonderful friends. I need and want nothing. I am beyond lucky and I am extremely grateful. I am safe, secure, and healthy. But, every so often envy slips into my psyche. I'm admitting it. I can still find myself listening to or watching others and wonder what I did wrong. Why didn't I make that choice; why didn't I travel that path; why do their lives appear so easy, so full? Sometimes it's little things that I find myself dwelling on; at other times, it's some major issue but, that doesn't serve me or anyone else. Whether I give credit to God, to fate, or to my own hard work for the life I now live, being ungrateful is plain wrong. By giving up ingratitude I found myself noticing when I undermine my own happiness and I stop and let it go. Perhaps by letting go of ingratitude for 46 days, I'll develop a new habit. Maybe by the end of Lent, I will rise to a new awareness, a new way of thinking about my life; a way that brings me and those in my life a sense of greater peace and joy.

I accepted the challenges presented to me for this season and decided that with my "free" time, I would pray more and listen harder. I believe that by embracing those steps I would open myself to God's grace and move forward in whatever direction I would be led. I decided not to be in charge and hoped that by focusing on my faith, on my relationship with Christ, I would be led to that place where it's not up to me how I use my time, treasure, and talent, but up to God. I believe that with the guidance of my Angels and Guides in those quiet moments, I am open to being used as their instrument.

Blessings and Friends

Affirmation: *I accept my friends and family as they are and I hold them in my daily prayers.*

There has been much written about how a social support system can bolster one's immunity. Not only do they increase our proclivity towards good health but they can increase our chances for a long, fulfilling life.

Relationships take work. Two people can meet and experience "love at first sight," but if that relationship is to survive, better yet thrive, it usually means it needs to be nurtured. Some friendships are low maintenance and others require a lot of effort. Friendships can wax and wane. How many people have you had in your life that seemed to just disappear? It's all a natural part of life although sometimes it can be hard to understand.

I've lived many different places and found myself almost completely on my own many times, especially those initial days after my husband and I had just moved. When we moved to Norwich, New York, in 1971 (population 7,000), I spent my first day in a motel room with our six-week-old daughter while my husband began his new job. The following weeks weren't much easier but this little town had a Newcomer's Club with child care that saved my sanity, if not my life. Some of those women (yes, we were all women) are still in my life, even though we moved away in 1976.

One of our moves took us to Cincinnati, Ohio. I felt like I'd landed on the moon. We arrived there with two small children. One of my first calls was to the local Newcomer's Club where I was informed I couldn't join because I wasn't living within their accepted boundaries. Such a club did not exist in my area. "Goodbye!" As I stood there wondering what I should do next I saw someone standing at the backyard gate.

She waved and a new friends entered my life. Her name was Shaun McLean. Thank God! At first I thought she was an angel and later in our relationship, I knew she was an angel.

While we were in Cincinnati one woman I met shared with me that she noticed some newcomers moving in down her street. I asked if she'd gone to meet them. "No," she replied, "I don't have time for any more people in my life." I was glad I hadn't moved by her. That's when I realized many of the people in our neighborhood felt the same way as that lady. It made me sad. It still makes me sad even though that was many years ago. When we moved from that community one of the neighbors said to me, "Moving again, honey?" We had been in our home almost ten years! The interesting part of this experience was that those neighbors who maintained a more open, adventurous approach to new relationships were truly remarkable people, many of whom became very dear friends and are to this day.

At the time of this writing we have lived in North Carolina for over twenty-five years. We'd been very active in the Triangle community, supporting, joining, and working for many organizations. We've been mostly blessed by the relationships and friendships we forged. I once heard a woman proclaim that once she stopped going to her children's school bus stop, she stopped making new friends. When I heard this pronouncement, I hadn't been to a school bus stop in over thirty years but by embracing life, trying new things, and staying committed to those I enjoyed, new and wonderful friends kept appearing. Both my husband, Sandy, and I embrace those good folks who open their lives, homes, and hearts to new relationships.

We need those relationships. We need to have people in our lives, other than family, who care for us and for whom we care. Each person in our life brings a different blessing. One may be someone you can go to with health issues, another someone with whom you play. Another may be of a similar spiritual proclivity, while another may not be and cause you to question and grow. One may be someone who likes to take a walk and another who likes to sit and talk. One may live close by and share in several of your activities and another may live far away and connects only periodically.

Sometimes we choose to end a friendship and at other times that ending is chosen for us. When there is a clear reason for the dissolution of the relationship, it can be easier to let go and move on, but when it remains a puzzle it can be much more difficult to disconnect. This rift can create a wound in the heart that may require a healing balm: prayer, counseling, or both. There is not always a clear vision of why someone has chosen to drop out of our lives. We can find ourselves wondering what we did when many times it had very little to do with us. I had a longtime friend who dropped me very suddenly and no matter how I reached out, there was absolutely no response. I couldn't imagine what I had done. Several months later I ran into a mutual friend of ours and was told she had stopped contacting him, too. Eventually, we found out that she was suffering from severe depression and had disconnected herself from everyone. It reminded me of calling someone on the phone and having them hang up on me as I stood there wondering what in the world I had done to cause such a reaction only to find out that they had an emergency taking place.

When a friendship saps your energy and is causing you to become unwell, it is time to end that relationship. It's never easy although the other person probably also recognizes there's a problem. When you have done all in your power to soothe the distress this relationship is causing but to no avail, it's probably time to walk away. It's usually best to let that person know you wish there was another way but for your well-being you need to separate. Even in our difficult friendships, however, there are blessings to be found. Many times those people who drive us crazy add to the fiber and the color of our lives. Perhaps they are the reason we are as strong and resourceful as we are; hopefully by dealing with that relationship we learned how to care for ourselves without holding onto any ill will.

My favorite friendships are those that develop because of similar interests and scheduled activities. They always seem like the easiest. These remind me of baking a cake. Once I've mixed all the ingredients and poured them into the pan, I simply have to put it in the oven and watch it rise. But, not all relationships afford us with those easy opportunities. Many of my friendships must be carefully nurtured to make sure they are sustained and continue to grow. I may have to do this by setting aside specific times to share a meal, perhaps it means an email or even an old fashioned letter (I love to send "snail-mail" birthday cards).

My goal is to maintain healthy, enriching friendships while also keeping enough energy to care for myself. It can be a very thin line especially with the availability of connecting via all the latest technologies like email, Facebook, and Twitter. It seems every day I decide how much energy is going into my relationships and how much I must reserve for myself. One way I do this is by praying daily for my friends, those far and near, those dear and daunting, those easy and challenging. I believe that my prayers will bless their lives. That way even if I'm not actively contacting them, they are in my thoughts and in God's hands. My intention is to value each friend for who they are and what they bring into my life. I'm not here to judge them. I am here to simply accept them and whenever possible to love and support them.

Imaginary Conversations

Affirmation: *I release myself from imaginary conversations.*

This affirmation was created during a visit to our mountain retreat. It's a small, two-bedroom condo in the North Carolina Mountains in a community called Hound Ears. It's called that because the two mountains it lies between look like dog ears, or so I am told. The condo looks out over the hills, a few ponds, and a pristine golf course. I journal in the morning while sitting on the porch. Many mornings I watch the mist rising from the hills as the sun begins its ascent. One morning there was a heron flying through the mist. I've put up a couple of potted plants containing petunias so that there is food for the hummingbird who visits. We have one dear friend who calls it Shangri-La, referring to the fictional place described in the 1933 novel *Lost Horizon* by British author James Hilton. Hilton describes Shangri-La as a mystical, harmonious valley. According to Wikipedia, Shangri-La has become synonymous with any earthly paradise but particularly a mythical Himalayan utopia: A permanently happy land isolated from the outside world. In *Lost Horizon*, the residents of Shangri-La are almost immortal, living years beyond the normal lifespan and only very slowly aging in appearance. Hound Ears is our Shangri-La and if you saw the number of healthy, hearty octogenarians and nonagenarians who reside here, you might think so too.

When I am in Hound Ears, I never want to leave, but unlike many of the residents who are retired and can come for six months, we are lucky if we get to stay for a few weeks. Most years we have a lot of family and friends come visit and we enjoy many moments of sharing time and making memories. Then, toward the end of our vacation we have some quiet time. It's a nice balance and gives me time to reflect, write, and pray. As the time to leave gets closer and closer, I have to use all my "tools" to help me to not "go home" early. I have to do all in my power to stay in the moment and to relish the present so that I don't leave this healing place before the actual time. Truly, it is a moment-to-moment meditation. As soon as I let go, my thoughts jump to home. Sometimes going home can mean I am returning to some challenging situations.

I've been guilty of having many imaginary conversations with many people. Why do I say guilty? Well, I am usually thinking about what I can say or what I would say or what I should have said or how about, what I could have said! If I'm reminiscing, I might ask myself what words would have been more effective? If I'm planning for the future, I might be wondering if I'll have the right words? Are there any words? Do I have the power to help someone else "see the light" or the power to make someone else go from being sad and anxious, to happy and calm? Can I say anything to improve and lighten another person's load?

Have you ever been here? Have you ever had a continuous one-way conversation over and over? The essence of suffering is wanting things to be different from the way they are and that's what I'm doing. I am creating my own suffering because I want to change the way another is perceiving something. Certainly, there are communication tools that can sometimes achieve this desired result but it can't happen if I only have the conversation in my mind. This kind of self-talk usually leads me to a very unsettled feeling. How can it not? There is no resolution. It never really ends. It's like a recording on repeat. It serves no purpose, does it? It takes one away from the moment. It takes me into my imagination and unless I choose to paint it, sculpt it, or write about it, it has no closure.

According to the Myers-Briggs personality test all of us fall either into the category of "introvert" or "extrovert." There is a range in each section so one's score can be high or low on the scale. These terms do not refer to how you relate to people but how you get your energy. An extreme introvert might need to be alone most of the time while an extreme extrovert might need to be out with people all the time. The category also refers to how one may communicate. The extrovert says exactly what they're thinking, when they're thinking it. The introvert ruminates on what they want to say, sometimes over and over, depending on the degree of introversion before they say anything. If you're not sure where you'd fall, ask yourself if you have to "practice" what you want to say before you make a phone call, especially a call involving something that requires a resolution. Your answer will give you some indication of whether you're an "E" or an "I." If you don't need to practice at all, you're a high "E." If you need to mentally go over it time and time again, you're a high "I."

I am a weak "I." I practice what I want to say but it depends on the situation. Sometimes, I can find myself practicing way too much. Mind you, I'm not practicing for the best. I am usually practicing for what I think will be an uncomfortable conversation. One of my other affirmations is: ***"The best is yet to come,"*** but when I'm facing some potential confrontation, it's really hard for me to call that one into existence.

When I began creating the affirmation about imaginary conversations, I found myself using the phrase "obsessive thoughts." I tried to release myself from obsessive thoughts that were becoming not just a conversation, but a saga. The longer I worked on letting them go, the more I realized they had become even more than that; I was developing an entire motion picture or a television mini-series! I found that what I really wanted to accomplish was to stop writing fiction, at least with regard to the issues I was facing when I would return home. I began writing, ***"I release myself from imaginary conversations and fully trust in God's loving care."*** I know I am much better off letting God write the story.

After several days of writing the affirmation in my morning pages, I began to feel my body relax. All the tension seeped away. What else did my new thought call to me? Mornings of journaling as I watch the mist rise from the hills, joy from the presence of the hummingbird as it flits around my planters, and an invitation to share my yoga practice with a friend who's looking for some calming tools. As I prepared for the session, I renewed several of my own peace-giving practices:

daily breathing rituals, guided meditations, gratitude-and-release sun salutations, and regular deep breaths.

My new affirmation brought peace, contentment, and a sated feeling. This was a perfect moment. I felt blessed and was resting in God's loving care. As the pastor, Fr. Christopher Gober, at St. Bernadette's in Linville, North Carolina, said in one of his homilies, "People, we have it all. We want for nothing." That's it, I want for nothing.

The Fabulous Female

Affirmation: *I treasure and celebrate my femininity.*

I was in my late twenties when I read *The Feminine Mystique* by Betty Friedan. I remember being stunned to find out there were other women who felt the same frustration I felt. I was not alone. I was already married and had one child and had left my teaching position and the only area of New York I had ever lived in and had followed my husband to a small town in upstate New York so that he could pursue his career. It seemed like a logical move. I had worked for a few years to help support our tiny family while he went to law school and finished his pharmacy certification. We now had a new baby and he had a new job and I was ready, I thought, for a new adventure. I didn't have a clue what I was getting myself into. Oh my! There I was in a new town and I knew no one, had a new baby and was unemployed. My husband left every morning for his job and it snowed all the time, 110 inches on the average every year.

It was the 1970s and the woman's movement was in full bloom but I was off in my own little world wondering what the heck was going on in my life. And then I met a few other women who were wondering the same thing and we began to talk about it and read about it. Oh, we didn't burn our bras or go out and picket the legislature, but there was a growing sense of awareness about where we now found ourselves but that we never had before explored. One of the elements of this self discovery was how many choices we now seem to have and also a certain sense that it wasn't enough to be "only" a wife and mother. This raised a lot of questions in my mind and also brought on a life-long struggle to find the best place for me to fully express myself; a place of balance between motherhood, wifedom and self-sufficiency. As I write this I feel I'm finally there, 40+ years later. It's been an interesting journey but finally, I've arrived.

March 8 of every year is International Woman's Day. March has now been officially declared International Woman's Month. I celebrated it in 2011, with over one hundred other women and at least one man. Sister Mary Margaret and Sister Judy from an organization called "A Place for Women to Gather" threw a party and what a wonderful event it was. There were all ages, races, sizes, and shapes and we had all come together to give thanks and praise for being a woman. It was a reminder of our grace and beauty and also of the price so many brave men and women paid for us to live the lives we are able to live today. Let's never forget the cost of the freedom we have. It wasn't that long ago that even here in the United States women couldn't vote, had limited availability to education, didn't receive equal pay for equal work, and weren't valued for their contributions to society.

This was a time to acknowledge and remember the abusive treatment of women that still exists in the world. It breaks my heart and makes my skin crawl when I read of or am told about the atrocities that so many women are subjected to in so many parts of the world. Don't think because you may not live in a third-world country that it isn't going on in your part of the world. It's going on around the corner, down the street, and maybe as close as next door. But, as far as we need to go to eliminate such abuse is as far as we have come. March is a special time to create awareness and to celebrate femininity. Don't forget the rights and privileges women have earned in such a short period of time and the price so many have paid to bring us to this place in time.

In my study group, one of the questions we asked ourselves was, "What other time and place would you have liked to live in, and would you prefer to be a man or a woman?" Think about it. What is your answer? We then had the opportunity to discuss what it was like to grow up as a woman in our families. I am the oldest in my family and my father desperately wanted a son. He didn't get one until ten years after I was born. I remember his joy. I was glad it took me so long to fully realize how important it was to him to sire a son. Up until then, I simply felt like the favored child and for some reason I felt I could do anything. But, society's restrictions were very heavy and I fell into the role somewhat expected of a young woman. The saving grace was St. Agnes Academic High School for women. The women there didn't know about limits. Many of my teachers had masters degrees and doctorates and many of my fellow students were looking at careers in medicine and government. I remember looking around and wondering why I wasn't pursing a college education, and because of their examples, I did just that. Without any help or guidance from anyone, I applied and was accepted to St. John's University and, because I didn't know any better, I applied to the mathematics program. There were five women in that program and about fifty men.

I'm a lucky woman—a very, very lucky woman—and I don't want to forget it. I am my own person. I get to choose all things in my life. I chose my path in life: education, religion, spouse, career, and my government officials, all because of the brave men and women who went before me. Now it is up to us to pave the way for the rest of the women in the world. What is the first step?

We must all, men and women, recognize and celebrate the gift of femininity. We must bring that feminine energy and spirit fully into the world. If you're a woman, claim your feminine power and beauty. Embrace fully your precious wisdom and sensuality. Know you are an amazing creation. You can bring forth life for heaven's sake! You are a miracle. If you're a man, honor your female relatives and friends. Let all the earth shout with joy, "This is woman; honor her and love her."

You Only Live Once

Affirmation: *Because I am open and accepting I am invited by family and friends to join them in fun experiences.*

"YOLO! YOLO! YOLO!" My teenage granddaughter, Isabelle, chanted when I told her I'd go to scuba diving lessons with her. It's so great having most of my family close by, especially my grandchildren. My granddaughter is a beautiful child inside and out. I'm very proud of her and of her mother's consistent guidance and influence. It's fun and educational to have someone her age in my life.

"What does YOLO mean?" I asked. I was told it's an acronym for You Only Live Once. This is not the first time she has brought me the gift of a new word or concept. She keeps me "in the loop" of current events and modern happenings. It's certainly not essential to my well-being but it's nice to have some knowledge of present day fads. "Grandma, would you go into a shark cage? " "Sure," I replied, "as long as it's not in the water." "You got me!" she smiled, and then we discussed small steps toward her goal of swimming with the sharks, "Maybe you should learn how to scuba dive first," I said. Her reply: "OK, will you go with me and learn too?"

Well, I'm somewhat claustrophobic, I must admit. I remember being in a tiny crowded elevator going up to the top of the Empire State Building and not being able to catch my breath. So, the thought of being strapped into a scuba suit and plunged into water is not very appealing. But, I've just been invited by my teenage granddaughter to join her on a great adventure. What would you say? "Sure," I replied and that's when she chanted "YOLO! YOLO! YOLO!" She went on to explain that it comes from a rap song done by someone named Drake and that I wouldn't like the rest of the song (I'll take her word for it). But, I love my new acronym and I love her.

I was also invited by my favorite (and only) daughter-in-law, Belen, to go with her to see her family in Ecuador. I have many reasons for not wanting to be in a third-world country where the economy is unstable and I don't speak the language, but I love the idea of immersing myself in the Spanish language and culture and I love my daughter-in-law. So, I said, "yes" to that invitation too.

I met a group of women many years ago all of whom were widows. They had traveled to the United States from Europe. They informed me that they never turned down an invitation. "If you stop saying yes, people will stop inviting you and life can become very lonely." I listened and made up my mind right then and there that I wasn't going to wait until I was a widow to accept the generous invitations of friends and family to join them in fun events.

I know we need to be discerning about our choices. We don't want to be human "doings." We want to weigh and carefully choose our options but if you're not open to the invitations, you might find there aren't that many choices out there for you. I'm speaking here about healthy choices not about choosing activities that are detrimental to your well-being. I'm not speaking about saying, "yes" to anything offered, like drugs or alcohol or other unhealthy activities. I'm talking about making your world smaller and smaller by letting fear or laziness or judgment keep you from trying new things, meeting new people, and having new experiences. I have had so many experiences in which I was hesitant to say yes but did and had some of the best times of my life.

Our family was once invited to a friend's lake house for a weekend and I didn't want to go. The thought about the amount of work it would take for me to prepare for the trip almost exhausted me before I even began. You'd think I would have already learned that it's all about the journey not the destination. It's about enjoying the moment not trying to predict the future or ruminating over the past. But, I knew, I truly knew, I would need to pack, buy food for ten people for three days, pick up the grandchildren and my mother, and do all the driving for almost two hours. Then, I'd have to unpack the car and make the beds, cook dinner, and then try to sleep in a strange bed in a strange place not to mention balancing all the personalities: four grandchildren ranging in age from 11 to 16, and my mom who was in her late 80s at the time, and Sandy, my husband, who hates the water—or at least has a much greater respect for its dangers than I.

For heaven's sakes! At the time I was 63 years old. I should have known by then what I wanted to do and didn't want to do, what would make me happy and what wouldn't. Just say, "No thanks, I don't want to do that." I have friends that wouldn't even consider taking on such an outing, but the invitation had come from some very dear friends and we don't get a lot of invitations to spend time in someone else's lake home. In fact, we'd never gotten an invitation like this before. "Come" they said, "bring the whole family." I felt an obligation to accept their generous offer.

I did it all, all the preparation. It wasn't nearly as daunting as I'd imagined. We arrived right after sunset. I walked out onto the deck and there was the full moon, so big it looked artificial. My heart and soul soared and tears filled my eyes, and for the next two days I had moments of the most exquisite joy. I felt like I was on drugs, the drugs of life. I was living life to the very fullest. It brought to my mind the poem: Life said, "Come to the edge." And I said, "No, I'm afraid. I'm weary." And, life demanded, "Come to the edge!" and so I went and life pushed me and I flew!

My husband, friends, and grandchildren windsurfed, kayaked, laughed, and played. My mother laughed and overcame her fear of riding in a speedboat for the first time. She was made to feel special and she loved being with everyone. I was filled to the brim with gratitude and joy!

One year my then six-year-old grandson went to away camp. He was so excited about going. I asked him why he was so excited and what he was most looking forward to. He told me he was excited about his new best friend. As far as I knew, he didn't know anyone else who was going to this camp. I asked him, "What new best friend?" "The one I'm going to make."

That's how I want to live life. I want to believe because I am open and accepting, my new best friend is out there waiting for me to meet, or that new adventure is out there waiting for me to experience. My granddaughter is right; Drake (whoever he is) is right. YOLO! YOLO! YOLO! This is it! This is our once in a life time opportunity. Don't let it pass you by. Say, "yes." Yes to life, yes to new experiences. Yes, yes, yes!

Keeping Out of the Cave of Phantoms

Affirmation: *When I stay focused on the present moment, my life is richer and less stressful.*

A trip looms in the future, a trip to another continent, a third-world country. I know how lucky I am to have this opportunity and I am excited about it but if I am I not vigilant, I walk into the "cave of phantoms" and it is both dark and frightening.

I am no stranger to fear and anxiety. I can clearly remember the first time it raised its ugly head and entered into my life. I was an older student returning to the University of North Carolina at Chapel Hill to obtain my master's degree in Social Work (MSW). I have never considered myself to be a gifted student. My accomplishments come more from a gift of perseverance and perhaps even the naive assumption that I can do anything if I decide to do it and stick to it. So, I took a bunch of baby steps to arrive in this master's program.

My first step was to sign up for a GRE review course. Other than the fee, there was nothing intimidating about it. I was simply going to see what I might learn. It was fun. So, I thought, "I'll take the exam. Why not?" and, to my amazement I did pretty well. "Well, I might as well apply to a program." I had a dear friend who had just earned her MSW and the subject was of great interest to me. I filled in the application for the part-time program and within a short period of time, I was accepted. I later learned they had hundreds of applications. They accepted 23 people and I was one of them. There I sat that first day with 22 other people all of whom seemed to have been in the field before. I had been a math major and a teacher. What was I doing here? But, I believed God had a plan for me. I didn't have a clue what it was but I was willing to be His/Her tool and it appeared a door had opened and I chose to step through. It took me five years to complete the degree, but I did it.

However, being back in school with all the tests, assignments, internships (62 credit hours), and final exams, took its toll on me. I would have days when I felt like I'd had ten cups of coffee but I hadn't. I'd awaken shaking inside and all the coping mechanisms that I'd developed over the years didn't seem to help in any way. I actually experienced several anxiety attacks but luckily for me I was studying exactly what I was dealing with and so I could easily diagnose myself and get help. Since then anxiety has visited me on (and fortunately) off many times. I see it. I know it but so often, I can do nothing to alleviate it except to know it will pass. Then I saw a television commercial about the end of the world.

The rumor was the world was ending (again) when the Mayan calendar ended, December 21, 2012. The commercial that shared this information was for retirement insurance and it pointed out that if the world ended as predicted, you wouldn't need insurance but just in case it didn't you might want to still be prepared.

I fully recognize that I am mortal. Besides being a cancer survivor and being an active part of both the Duke Cancer Patient Support and the Preston Robert Tisch Brain Tumor advisory boards, I was a Hospice patient care volunteer and did my first MSW internship with Hospice of Wake County. I lost my father when I was 34 and all of these factors have combined to create in me a heightened sense of awareness that I may be only one breath away from the next life. I try to keep that thought with me at all times for both myself and for my loved ones.

So, when the insurance commercial came on it really made an impression on me. I don't know why, perhaps it was simply the way it was portrayed. It was whimsical and silly but it also presented a very real possibility. We are spinning through space on one of billions of planets among billions of solar systems. We've all seen the disaster movies about comets hitting the earth or the sun getting too close or too far or our axis slightly tilting and sending us all floating into outer space. It's true. Any day now the planet could implode or even more likely, we could die in a car crash or some other common accident.

If you ever get a chance, visit the Newseum in Washington, DC. It is six floors of everything pertaining to the news as it was and as we now know it. It's filled with fascinating exhibits and interactive experiences. On the main floor is the antennae from the top of the south building of the World Trade Center, and on the wall are the front pages of all the major newspapers announcing the events of September 11, 2001. That alone is a reminder that we don't have a clue what's facing us from moment to moment, no less far out into the future.

The Buddha tells us to "imagine the glass broken." He reminds us that life as we know it is fragile and temporary. It's not morbid. It brings us a greater realization of the preciousness of what we have. We need to treasure it.

Now whenever anxiety arises I think only of the present moment. I completely let go of the unknown or perhaps the dreaded future. Why should I be anxious or worry about something that may never take place? Not that I will necessarily die and my future will end but I can only plan for whatever it is I want to happen; after that my future and my days are in the hands of God. I haven't got a clue what they will bring and because of that thought, I find myself at peace. The anxiety seeps away. I recall Shakespeare, "Cowards die many times before their deaths; the valiant never taste of death but once." Yes, I may be here for another 30 years or more. The world may last for centuries to come but none of that is any concern of mine. The future is just that: A world unknown. I will not allow myself to be afraid of the phantoms I may never meet.

May All Your Dreams Come True

Affirmation: *By pursuing my dreams I help to make the world a better place.*

The newspaper article was about an organization called "Wish of a Lifetime." It explained it isn't the only organization of its type. There is also The Twilight Wish Foundation, The Bucket List foundation, Forever Young Senior Wish Organization, and S.H.O.W. (Seniors Having One Wish). They all have the same goal: To grant a wish to an elderly person who is in desperate need of a morale booster. The article's photo was of centenarian Miriam Krause. She was shown in the basket of a hot air balloon. She had requested a ride for her 100th birthday.

How do you feel about seeing dreams come true? One of my prayers for my children is for "true dreams." My husband's philosophy regarding a parent's happiness is, "On any given day most parents are as happy as their unhappiest child." When he first shared this with me, our children were teenagers. As I write this, they are adults and that philosophy is as true today as it was then. Therefore, it is in my best interest to pray that their dreams come true. Now I have added my grandchildren. Actually, my daily prayers request God's "favor and blessings" on everyone for whom I pray, those I pray for by name and those in the world "who most need Your mercy."

Do you have a bucket list? In case you need help putting one together there are all sorts of websites that have lists on them to help you along. One such site is Bucketlist.org. It actually offers "10,000 things to do before you die." The first time I heard the term "Bucket List" was from the 2007 movie by the same name starring septuagenarians Jack Nicholson and Morgan Freeman. As of this writing, Jack Nicholson and Morgan Freeman are still going strong and I would imagine there isn't much on their personal lists that they have missed.

I was surprised that it's fairly common for teenagers to have bucket lists. My granddaughter, Isabelle, has one. So far, I think the fun for her is discovering those things she wants to add to the list. Certainly, I hope she has as long as Jack or Morgan to work on checking off her dreams.

Our dream list can be very different at different times just like our prayer list. In times of peace, our dreams can be very specific, like a new house or a vacation or perhaps time to enjoy our favorite activity. When my husband and I went on a tour of the Ryman Auditorium in Nashville, we were paired with another couple. The Ryman is the original home of the Grand Ole Opry. As we were escorted into Johnny Cash's dressing room, I noticed the gentleman on the tour with us became very quiet. He almost looked like he couldn't catch his breath. I looked at him with concern when his wife spoke, "This is his dream come true. He has always wanted to see the Ryman and where Johnny Cash had his dressing room." I loved being in this place with this man when he realized one of his dreams.

In times of strife, our dream list can be more universal. Our dream may be for a world filled with peace, good health, and safety for all. For me the greatest dreams are those that will improve the world's conditions. Of course one cannot deny that when an individual makes his or her dream come true, the world does become a better place. But, when I see and read about those people who dream really big and bring them into reality, I am awed. In the same newspaper issue that had the "Wish of a Lifetime" story, there was also a story about the problem of hunger in the United States. It highlighted several organizations that glean[3] food. "Volunteers descend on farm fields and reclaim some of the estimated seven billion pounds of fresh produce left in the fields or sent to landfills each year, recovering it for the plates of millions who can't afford it," according to Chuck Raasch of *USA Today*. Many of the volunteers are school-aged children. Gleaning is not something new. It was practiced as far back as biblical times. I like to imagine, however,

---

[3] Glean: "to gather grain or other material that is left after the main crop has been gathered" (Merriam-Webster)

that the modern creation of gleaning was someone's dream. They saw the waste and decided to gather it up to feed the hungry.

My church, Saint Michael the Archangel in Cary, has a sister parish in Honduras. Each year we contribute to the needs of the people in that parish. We provide books and clothing for children, build buildings, provide medicine, and the ability to acquire clean water. A team of parishioners travel there each year to do whatever they can for the sister parish. When I was at the John C. Campbell Folk School, Patricia Sprinkle, author and creative writing teacher, shared the story of her journey to India to teach creative writing to the "untouchables" and of her work in the Church of the Brethren with whom she led a group to help children in Louisiana after Hurricane Isaac. Thank God! These are just a few examples of the good people are doing by pursuing their dreams.

Of course, one need not look to or go to a foreign country to make a positive difference. Every day people walk out their front doors and head off to help others. Our volunteers can be found in hospitals, homeless shelters, food banks, and schools, to name just a few. I had the dream of creating a yoga retreat for breast cancer survivors and from that dream came the Pink Ribbon Yoga Retreat.[4]

Organizations that are born from the dream of someone who wants to make a difference in our world must also be part of God's dream: to end abuse, cure cancer, bring solace to the suffering, provide food to the hungry, give shelter to the homeless. The dreams of a higher order and each individual who steps out to add to the comfort, to bring "favor and blessings" to another are part of the vision our world so desperately needs.

There are so many dreamers in our world. What's one of your dreams? So many dreamers have made their dreams reality. Whether it's a trip to a far-away place, a new charitable endeavor or a ride in a balloon, it's important to pursue our dreams. Yes, each time a dream comes true the world becomes a brighter place and isn't that exactly what the world needs: more joy and more light?

---

[4] http://www.pinkribbonyoga.org/

Claiming Your Power

Affirmation: *I stand in my power.*

How many women do you know who would say they love themselves? It seems to me that most women have a lot of difficulty valuing themselves. Most of the discussions I have with my female friends and attendees at my workshops are about ways to increase our self-esteem, especially as we grow older.

The intention I set for my individual yoga practice and any class I teach is to "nurture and empower." I believe that a regular yoga practice is one of the tools that will help us develop and encourage us to deepen both of those qualities. Some yoga poses allow us to rest and let gravity hold us while we slowly release more deeply into the pose. I feel that way when I do Child's pose, or *balasana*. In this pose you kneel down, sit back onto your heels, place your forehead on the floor and rest your arms, hands up, along the side of your body. As you breathe, your whole back stretches open from the bottom of your spine up to the top. Your legs and feet loosen up and your shoulders relax into the ground. There is also *savasana*, or Corpse pose. It's the last pose in most practices; you lie flat on your back (if this is comfortable for you), hands placed palms up at your sides and allow gravity to hold you while you continue to keep the mind free of the clutter of life. I always remind my students that this is a very important pose because as one of my mentors, Nancy Hannah, taught me "Mindful movement followed by stillness brings healing to the mind, body, and spirit."

When I practice and when I teach, my mission is to also empower. There are many poses which can encourage a sense of strength and power. One of the poses that is frequently included in most practices is *virabhadrasana*, Warrior pose. There are three main Warrior poses. The tale surrounding these poses is that a young woman was deeply wounded by her father and decided to shed her body. While in a meditative state, her body burst into flames. When her husband, the god Shiva, heard of her death he called on his fiercest warrior and named this warrior, Virabhadra (Vira (hero) + Bhadra (friend)). He then ordered Virabhadra to go and avenge his wife's death, which Virabhadra did. Nowhere in the story does it say if the warrior is a man or a woman. You get to choose. When you take a stance for Warrior I, you spread your legs apart, both feet pointing forward, the back foot a little turned out, then bend your front knee, face forward and raise your straight arms overhead. You ground your feet and you lift your torso. In Warrior II, you take the same basic stance, but you turn your torso to the side, place your arms in a "T" position, palms down, and gaze out over the front hand. It looks like you're preparing to throw a spear or a javelin. In Warrior III, you stand on one leg and your other leg is stretched back and it and your torso and usually your arms are parallel to the ground, like you're about to swing out and kick something. Practicing any one of these stances will elicit a feeling of power in mind, body, and spirit.

A diagnosis and treatment plan for cancer or some other life-threatening illnesses can be a very disempowering experience. Many in the medical field in an attempt to help you save your life forget that you still need to be in charge. They may need a reminder that you are more than willing to partner with them in your health care but you are not going to allow them to take over your whole life. Claiming your power in this instance can be the difference between life and death. If you have a feeling that the caregiver you are working with is not on your team, it is imperative that you resolve the conflict or find a new caregiver. Follow your instincts and claim your power. Before I began treatment for breast cancer, I decided to practice my *virabhadrasana* poses. I decided I needed to take a "Warrior" stance in order to prepare myself for the cancer process. I found a counselor with the Duke Cancer Patient Support Program. I then gathered my troops about me and got all the information I could find about other steps people have successfully used to empower themselves through this experience: a nutritionist, an acupuncturist, a massage therapist, and most importantly, my prayer groups. I invited and allowed any friend who wanted to help me through cancer to help me in any way that suited them. Truly, I entered into that first chemo session fully armed. I had my family, doctors, nurses, and technicians to guide the meds and treatment and I had prayers, information, meditation tapes, and a *USA Today* crossword puzzle. I was fully prepared for battle.

The first time I heard someone tell me they needed to "stand in their power" I knew immediately what she meant. Sometimes it's too easy to think small. It's too easy to feel small, to let things go unresolved so that someone's feelings are not ruffled. That, however, can become a habit that only diminishes our power and our spirit. Years ago when I was a very young woman there were courses designed to help people become more assertive, not aggressive, they would stress, but assertive. Mostly these courses were attended by women. What determines whether or not a woman feels powerful—or not—or for that matter how anyone feels about themselves? I'm sure the first criteria is childhood experiences. Were these people led to believe they were special, smart, gifted? Were they encouraged to follow their hearts and their imagination, or were they treated poorly (or worse, abused)? Even after such spirit-damaging treatment, however, many people go onto find their self worth.

Steve Jobs, founder of Apple, died in October of 2011. He changed the face of information technology and the way the world saw and used all sorts of devices. One of the stories I read about Steve Jobs is that as a child, when confronted by another child about his adoption, he became very upset. The other child asked him how it felt to know he was abandoned by his birth parents. His adopted parents gave the perfect answer to his question of abandonment. They explained to him that they had chosen him from all the other children in the world. For most of us, that would be enough to help us feel better and to value ourselves. Steve Jobs took it to a whole new level. He said from that moment on he knew he was not abandoned; he was Chosen!

As women age in our society, traditionally their value is diminished. Older women are not normally looked upon as favorably as older men. Just look at our older actors versus our older actresses. Even if in America you don't find a lot of older women in the movies, thank heavens for the British and Dames Maggie Smith, Helen Mirren, and Judi Dench. It seems to me that the values our society holds up as a reflection of "success" are normally male-held values. I do believe, however, that is changing. Women today seem to be able to stay true to themselves and still find worldly success. Let's face it, sadly we still don't have many women officially leading the countries of the world. We have had, however, many women warriors who have led our society out of darkness and into the light: Mother Teresa, Eleanor Roosevelt, Susan B. Anthony, Rosa Parks, and Helen Keller, to name just a few. We do have many more women in professions that were once consider strictly male territory. When I majored in mathematics in college, I was one of five women in a program of about fifty men. No more! We now have women leading the fields of medicine, science, law, and politics but perhaps some of your heroines aren't on this list. What of our mothers, sisters, friends, and mentors? They may be the women you think of when you think of powerful, strong women.

What if you believed that everything you do, everything you say, every thought you have, has an influence on everyone else in the world? Would you think of yourself as powerful? I am here to tell you that that is true! Our simple presence in this world affects everyone else and everything else that exists. We are interwoven in ways we cannot even fathom. There is a network of energy that runs from each of us to each other. Therefore, we have a responsibility to value ourselves and each other. We have a responsibility to claim our power. We must all believe in ourselves. We must! We must recognize and value our contributions, our existence. Men and women alike need to know without doubt that we have value, each of us, and it's especially important to claim it as we age. We need to recognize and take credit for the way we have made life better; it will affect every aspect of our life and every person we encounter. When you truly claim your power and let your light shine, you give permission to the rest of world to do the same.

What do you think your life would be like if you believed that you were chosen? What would it take for you to believe that you are

Creating Positive Affirmations, Living an Intentional Life

powerful? What tools can you use to ensure that as you move forward you will know that simply because you are, you are important; you are a force with which to be reckoned. One of the first tools is to stand up and tell yourself, "I am powerful! I stand in my power! I claim my power!" Yes, we are chosen, each and every one of us. We have been chosen by the greatest Father of all.

Claim your power. Say it! Write it! Watch how your body responds. An affirmation can feel strange at first but don't give up, keep with it and one day if you're not there already, you'll be in a place where you find yourself standing tall, feeling strong and you'll know without a doubt that you are valued, you are important, you are loved.

Fun!

Affirmation: *I have fun, fun!*

My affirmation used to be, "I have fun, fun, fun!" But I was actually having too much fun. I could exhaust myself running from activity to activity, so I took off one of the "funs." This may seem like a silly, trite affirmation but this one developed from the advice and example of a very dear friend and fellow breast cancer survivor, Anna Moore. No matter what she was going through in her life she always focused on the fun; she focused on the upside of the challenges. She is inspirational in the way she attacks her experiences with joy and hope.

When I went for tests to prepare for chemotherapy treatments, I had a young male technician ask me why I was undergoing the tests and when I shared with him that I was beginning chemo on Wednesday for breast cancer he said, "Boy, I hope you're doing something fun on Thursday." I can still hear his voice and remember my shocked response. I was just getting ready. I hadn't really planned for anything afterwards. To be honest, I was wondering if I'd even be able to get out of bed afterwards no less plan for something fun. That one statement , however, sent me on a remarkable journey.

What was it that brought me joy? What did I like to do that was fun? Well, I had a list but my favorite thing was to invite my friends to my home for lunch or dinner. I'd have an after-chemo luncheon! With the help of a dear friend, we sent out invitations to all those people who had reached out to me when they heard about my diagnosis. We invited them to lunch at my home and we invited them to bring a dish to share. Yes, I had several calls and messages asking me if I was sure about this decision, and a couple of people who told me I was crazy, but I assured them that this was what I wanted to do.

Seventy-five people showed up for what was to be the first of four after-chemo luncheons. I was not feeling my best (to put it mildly) but I was having company and I needed to pull myself together and greet my guests and receive all the hugs and warm wishes they had brought with them. It was a marvelous event! I invited my then yoga teacher, Donna Plock, to open with some yogic breathing (*pranayama*) and meditation. At each luncheon someone shared a meditation or a story with the group and helped us bless the food and the gathering before we came together to eat, visit, and celebrate the healing process that I was undergoing. At the last three luncheons, I was bald and I was suffering some of the other effects of the treatments ... but it didn't matter. I was surrounded by all these amazing people who had taken their time and energy and had chosen to come support me during this major life challenge.

Very few men came to the luncheons, although they were always included in the invitations. I can clearly recall the ones who chose to brave the onslaught of women attendees and step into a situation that is mostly female. One of them was my brother, Frank Grolimund. To my complete surprise, he and his wife, Diane, drove down from another state. This is one of the many gifts I gave myself when I decided to share my journey and my life with those who had shown me love and concern.

The question asked on that day of tests by that wonderful technician completely turned around my breast cancer treatment from scary and onerous to one that was nurturing and yes, fun! If one can turn chemo and radiation into a fun experience, I think one may only need to put two "funs" into her or his affirmation. In fact they may only need one "fun." How many do you want in your affirmation? What's something you are facing with trepidation that you might be able to turn around by finding some aspect that you can call "fun"?

Hope is a Choice

Affirmation: *The best is yet to come.*

"Can you get to a place where you believe your best is in front of you?" This is the question John Ramsey was asked by a friend years after the death of his daughter, six-year-old beauty pageant queen JonBenet Ramsey. In 1996, she was found dead in the basement of his home in Boulder, Colorado, and the murder has never been solved. There has been an enormous amount written about the case. He and his (now-deceased) wife were the target of the investigation for quite a while and were eventually cleared of the charges, but for many doubts still linger. He has written a book about his years of grief and recovery, *John Ramsey's Journey from Grief to Hope*.

I don't normally follow the sordid details of such stories but just by being alive and keeping up with current events, it was impossible not to know something about this sad story. Certainly, I knew only the hearsay evidence to which I'd been exposed and in my heart I wanted to believe in his innocence. What I was struck with during his interview with Robin Roberts on Good Morning America was how very sad and tragic this entire story is. It made my heart ache.

But, back to the question; I'm sure it's one many of us could ask ourselves at many times in our lives. We have or are going through a really difficult time or a challenging experience, and we can't see any light at the end of the tunnel. We think this is it. Life will always be this grim and difficult. What does it take to find the ability to turn that around? Hope.

There have been times in my life when hope was missing and who's to say that that won't happen again. But, it's so wonderful to be with people who give and share their hope when everything looks dark. Have you had that experience? Both my father, Frank Grolimund and my father-in-law, Joe Costa, died of brain tumors, the same rare type (a glioblastoma), twenty years apart. I had hope with my Dad, but at the time I knew so little. When my father-in-law was diagnosed, I gave up immediately. I knew the results. I'd already experienced them. Joe, however, was being treated (at Duke Hospital's) Preston Robert Tisch Brain Tumor Center by Doctors Henry and Alan Friedman[5]. The motto of the center is "At Duke there is hope." It was inspirational to be with the people who worked there. They really believed they could cure him. They believe they can find a way to eliminate this disease, and while my father-in-law died, so many more have lived—and thrived. There are many stories of people who are living long and wonderful lives because there are people at Duke who believe that they can make a difference ... and who have made a difference.

Hope is a feeling of positive expectation. Can one go from despair to hope? Yes, I believe they can. How can one go from despair to hope? Sometimes we can try it alone but at other times we may need others to help us. I remember a woman who was going through breast cancer treatment telling me that if her friends hadn't pulled her up out of the dark pit she was in, she didn't think she'd ever have gotten out. But, hope is also something we can develop, like a muscle. We can practice it when we're not in such dire straits. We can practice believing, **"The best is yet to come."**

The book *The Emotional Life of Your Brain* (Richard J. Davidson with Sharon Begley) focuses on "The New Science of Feelings," the study of the neurological basis of emotions. The book cites an example of the brain's neuroplasticity (changes in neural pathways and synapses due to changes in behavior, environment and neural processes) with the example of virtuoso musicians, whose portion of the brain tied to finger movements is larger than average. In the book, the author refers to a study in which (non-professional musician) adults were asked to pretend to practice the piano for several weeks. These subjects experienced growth in that same part of the brain.

---

[5] No relation to one another.

Therefore, as adults we can still change the condition of our brain if we choose. I know with the epidemic condition of Alzheimer's many of us are concerned with the health of our brains, or those of our loved ones. It was once believed that adult brains were fixed and permanent, and change could not take place. It's nice to know "they" were wrong. Once again it shows the power of choosing and creating our thoughts. We can expand those parts of our brains that support our desires to live more positive lives. Remember: That which you think about, you bring about. We can choose to tell ourselves, ***"The best is yet to come,"*** and rest in the knowledge that our brains are receiving that message, our bodies are responding, and our innermost desires are being completely supported.

Gratitude and Forgiveness

Affirmation: *I have an attitude of gratitude in All things.*

Thank You! Thank You! Thank You! (TYTYTY for short) Two weeks after I received a "gratitude and forgiveness" message it was still coming in strong. It didn't matter where I turned, the message was there. I opened two emails I regularly receive and there it was. I read my daily readings and again, there it was and then, I watched a homily on television and once again, the message was "praise God in ALL things." I took this to mean that I still have a lot of work to do, and since I am determined to release all resentment from within and to live a Christ-centered life of peace, love, joy, gratitude, and compassion, I am fully open to any and all the messages the Universe sends me. I was surprised it had taken me this long to recognize this message.

I've been saying the Lord's Prayer since I learned to talk. I'll bet I've said, "And forgive us our trespasses as we forgive those who trespass against us," a million times. It's a simple message, but it's not an easy message. Obviously, it's a very important one. Of all the things Christ taught us, this was a priority. Was I just saying the words and never listening to the message? Was I ready now to fully embrace this concept? I was. This, however, is not something I could do on my own. I believe this requires a healing of the spirit, and for me that demands I turn it completely over to God, to Jesus Christ. Once again I am faced with a simple concept, but a difficult life skill. I am asked not to forget, but to forgive. The world can be a dangerous place. There are a lot of terrible things going on. Many people suffer great injustices. How do we let go of those experiences and find the blessings in them? It is possible? I believe it's only possible with supernatural assistance.

I once heard Dennis Covington, the author of *Salvation on Sand Mountain*, speak. He was a reporter at the time and his assignment was to visit the churches that had the practice of handling snakes. It says in Mark 16:17–18 (NIV[6]) "They will pick up snakes with their hands; and when they drink deadly poison, it will not hurt them at all ..." He got caught up in the whole practice and eventually wrote the book. What I remember most about his story is the question he asked, "What if you truly believed?"

What would you be willing to do? What would you feel you could do if you truly believed? What kind of faith is that? After much thought I came to the conclusion that we all have snakes to handle. What if our faith were strong enough that we believed those poisonous "snakes" of cancer, heart disease, abuse, violence, depression and anxiety, betrayal, and abandonment could do us no harm? What if our faith were so strong that we could not only trust that God had a plan for our lives, but also handle it and be grateful for it, without being bitten or poisoned?

I know this is an expansion on what the religious snake handlers believe, but I decided that the message is about the strength God gives us should we choose to believe. It's not about the snakes; it's not about what's happening outside of us; it's all about what's happening inside of us. It's how we perceive the dangers and troubles of this life. It's not about what happens to us. Stuff happens. It's about how we perceive what happens to us and we are called, for our own sake and the sake of others, to be grateful for all things and to forgive at all cost.

When my friend, Carrie Aaron, visited me she brought with her the gift of TYTYTY and the message of letting go of all resentment and embracing total forgiveness. She shared a meditation she uses throughout her day. She graciously agreed to let me share it with you here:

> *Breathe deeply, close your eyes and imagine your crown chakra opening up. Send white light (perhaps the healing light of the Holy Spirit) through your crown chakra down through your brain, then filling your sinus cavity, mouth, throat, down and filling your shoulders, chest cavity,*

---

[6] New International Version

stomach. Take time in filling your hip area with the white light, then down through your legs and feet, down to the center of the Earth. Now you're connected by the light from Heaven to the center of the Earth. Gently open your heart chakra and let the light fill your heart; now the love and energy from your heart mixes with the white light. Now feel the emotion of gratitude. Say, "TYTYTY" over and over; turn up the volume; make the pictures brighter; magnify your gratitude tenfold. Make a bubble of that mixed energy (white light, heart energy, gratitude) the size of your heart. Now expand the bubble around you, marinate in the energy for a bit. Now expand the bubble to the size of the room you are in. Then expand to as large as you want. Then gently open your eyes, notice how much brighter the colors are, how shapes have more dimension, and how smells are stronger. Take this vibration of 1,000 with you the rest of the day. Repeat as often as needed throughout the day.

May you find the "tools" that enable you to fill all your days with peace, love, joy, gratitude, and compassion.

The Power of Prayer

Affirmation: *I pray unceasingly.*

Do you believe that prayer makes a difference? Do you have a theory about why it does or doesn't work? Have you ever "tested" your theory?

The older I become the more I pray and the more I value prayer. I once heard a comedian say that's very normal because as we age we realize we're getting closer to death and we're "hedging our bets." That could very well be true.

I begin my day before I even rise with a prayer of thanksgiving and with an invitation to God to join me throughout my day and to bring blessings and favors on all those for whom I have promised to pray. I pray for my spouse, my children, and grandchildren by name and then go on and list my siblings and their families. Next, I include all my "dear, dear friends" and "especially those who most need God's mercy." I try to recall each of those special people by name whom I know need extra prayers. I can usually remember them. If not, I do keep a prayer list. After my friends I include all "the special intentions of those in my Small Christian Community." I then go on to add "all the support people in my life, seen and unseen, and their loved ones." I so value all those people who make my life so much easier and richer because of their hard work. I include our "fighting men and women and their families" and finally I pray for "wisdom for our world leaders and peace for this world." Then, it is time to rise.

Am I making a difference? I'm making a difference in how I value those in my life and how I perceive them and the world. I sometimes think this aspect is the most powerful effect of prayer; the change that takes place in me when I take the time and spend my energy to pray for others. I believe prayer makes a difference in ways we cannot even fathom. It is one of the most powerful tools available to us to tap into the Divine. If we are spiritual beings having a human experience, why not connect with spirit and let that power work the miracles we are asking for in our lives?

According to Norman Vincent Peale in *The Power of Positive Thinking*, the whole world is made up of vibrations and prayer is one way to activate and send out positive vibrations to create change in the world. The direction and control of positive energy has been written about in numerous books, including those of Eckhart Tolle and Gary Zukav. That's what prayer is: It's a form of energy. Several years ago Duke Medicine did a study on prayer. They had two groups prayed for by a variety of people from all different religious theologies. The results of their study did not show any difference in the recovery of the patients. I wonder, however, what did change for those who were receiving the prayers? Do you think it might have been something that wasn't measurable like grace, peace, hope, and other non-tangibles?

I firmly believe that prayer changes lives. The greatest challenge is believing in its power; believing that it really can have an effect on a situation. The second challenge is believing that it will be a positive effect even if it's not the apparent answer for which we prayed. Prayer, belief, and the ability to tap into the Divine do not remove our difficulties but can make our difficulties and challenges easier to bear. They can bring us a sense of peace and hope believing that there is a kind and loving Supreme Being who wants what's best for us, especially if we're willing to ask and then to listen.

When we first moved to North Carolina, I said a prayer that God would lead us to the best house and neighborhood for us and I asked for a "sign." I asked for some sort of burning bush. Yes, I was testing. Well, we drove everywhere and I never saw that bush. We finally settled on a lovely house in a new neighborhood and I let go of my search for the perfect place for us. I actually loved our new home and our new neighbors, so all was good. Several years later, we were taking my in-laws around showing them the area and we saw a beautiful house that was for sale. We were able to tour it on the spot and I loved it! Soon, we had sold our other house and moved into the new one. One day, I was walking with someone who knew a lot about shrubs and he was telling me about the different bushes around the house. I stopped dead when he pointed to the bushes at the bottom of the driveway and told me they were called "Burning Bushes" (*euonymus alatus*). There were six of them! Was that answered prayer? As far as I was concerned, it was.

I don't go around testing God any longer. I simply expect my prayers to be answered. I know they are answered and I know they make a difference, a difference in my life and a difference in the world but I must remind myself that God's plan may not be my plan and that God's timing is something I will never be able to fathom.

SUMMER

Dancing for Life

Affirmation: *I smile early, laugh daily, dance often.*

In most cultures dance is an integral part of life. Here in the United States one must make a greater effort to find the opportunity to dance. At this point in time however, it seems like the media has had more of a focus on dance than it has had in the past. For example, there's *Dancing with the Stars* and *So You Think You Can Dance*. Even some of our finest athletes, Olympic medal winners, have shown an interest in dancing. When Ryan Lochte, the 2012 winner of twelve Olympic swimming medals was interviewed on Good Morning America, he said he would like the opportunity to compete on *Dancing with the Stars*. Hope Solo, the 2012 goalie for the US Women's soccer team, competed on *Dancing with the Stars* in 2011 and in 2007 the Olympic speed skating gold medalist Apolo Ohno danced his way to the Mirror Ball Trophy.

Now too, we have all sorts of dance exercise. The gym I attend, Rex Wellness of Cary, has had a Latin dance class for many years and of course there's aerobics, which usually has some sort of upbeat tunes. As of this writing, Zumba has become very popular and most yoga classes have music in the background.

Yoga is not normally thought of as a form of dance exercise, but I have always felt the vibrations and the rhythm of the music as I practiced the *asanas*. When I trained at Kripalu Center for Yoga and Healing, we had several wonderful classes that included live drum music. The Dance Yoga concept (formerly Dance Kinetics) was actually developed at Kripalu. At the Pink Ribbon Yoga Retreat, a yearly beach-yoga retreat for breast cancer survivors, Saturday evenings are celebrated with Yoga Dance.

At the time of this writing, TJ Martin, one of our gifted yoga teachers and a founding member of the retreat, has led us in Yoga Dance for the last nine years. Of course, there are many different reactions to our dance event. Some, but not all, like myself, can't wait.

In *The Artist's Way*, Julia Cameron asks you to imagine what you would like to do if you had several other lives. It's a fun exercise to see what you might be missing that you could actually do in this life. I would have loved to be more actively involved in the world of dance. There have been times in my life when the music led me to total abandonment. I love going shopping with my granddaughter, Isabelle, because she'll just smile if she sees me dancing about the store to some broadcasted tune (unlike my children, who I am sure were mortified by their mother's lack of decorum).

Many of the women who come to the Pink Ribbon Yoga Retreat have been there before but everyone has had that initial introduction to our evening of Yoga Dance. TJ has always done a marvelous job of explaining how the session is structured. She explains that each of the songs are designed to open one of the seven Chakras, energy centers of the body. A yoga practice with or without dance can aid in opening the energy centers. The seven Chakras begin at the base of the spine, the Root Chakra, and run through the body to the top of the head, the Crown Chakra. Envision a stream of energy or light, moving up through your body, flowing freely, keeping everything open and clean and soft. Ancient yoga tradition teaches when the Chakras are opened and aligned, we are balanced and in a state that encourages optimal health.

TJ brings some props, including feather boas and mesh scarves. Some of the women bring coin skirts. At one retreat two of the returning ladies came to the evening session a little late. They attempted to come in quietly so as to not disturb the group, but they wore their coin skirts and had added bell bracelets and anklets. They also were in full flowing skirts and had silk flowers in their hair. The fun had begun!

TJ typically begins our Yoga Dance evening by inviting us to sit on our mats. We move slowly at first. One of the songs for the first chakra is "Breathe." Then she invites us to stand up and we move to songs like "Feeling Good" by Michael Bublé. Then the energy begins to increase and for the third chakra we get to dance to songs like "Shake Your Body" and "New Attitude." The next set of songs include songs like "We Are Family," "Walk of Life," "You Raise Me Up," and "Loka Samasta." Can you hear it? Can you feel it? Finally, we're ready to wind down and we do that to songs like "The Empty Sky."

Yoga Dance is one of the healing modalities we offer for the retreat. One year one of our attendees did not seem to connect with anyone or anything that was being offered. We would find her sitting in the living room watching television while everyone else was participating in one of the activities. She wasn't very interested in the art projects and her favorite yoga pose was *savasana* (the final resting pose in a yoga practice). But during Yoga Dance, when we reached the songs for the third Chakra, it happened. I was directly across from her when the music began and it was one of the most astonishing things I have ever seen: a grin came to her face, she lit up from within and she began to dance with total abandonment. She didn't stop until we were ready to lie down. Her enthusiasm and love of music took her to a place during the retreat that nothing else was able to accomplish. From then on, she was an integral part of the group. People took the time to tell her how much they enjoyed watching her and dancing with her.

There have also been women who refused to dance. I try not to judge but I wasn't always successful. But if they return, sooner or later (sometimes years later) something happens and I will look up and there they will be moving and smiling, and many times laughing. It is so very joyful. It is so very healing.

I believe we can enhance our health by sometimes tricking our bodies to think we are feeling good. I once read a story about a man who played the music for silent films. He was asked if it was hard to play music that went with the feelings of the scenes. He answered he didn't concern himself with that. The music he chose created the emotions the viewers experienced.

If you're sad and you don't want to be, smile. If you're feeling blue and you don't want to be, laugh. If you want to fully embrace life and go a little crazy turn on the music and dance.

"Dance as though no one is watching you,
Love as though you have never been hurt before,
Sing as though no one can hear you,
Live as though heaven is on earth."
Dr. William W. Purkey

Who Are These People?

Affirmation: *I am audacious. I say, "Yes, I can!"*

When Geraldine Lucas was 58 years old she climbed the Grand Teton Mountain. Originally from the East coast, she had retired as a teacher and packed herself up and established a homestead in Wyoming in what is now the Grand Tetons National Park. In the beginning she didn't even have electricity or running water! It appears from the stories I was told while traveling through the area that the women back then were very influential in the development of this state and in its governing.

The brave, adventurous spirit must continue to thrive in this part of the world because wherever my husband, Sandy and I traveled in Wyoming, we found people with an amazing sense of adventure. Pink's name tag had "Taiwan" printed under her name. She was a waitress in Yellowstone National Park. I was in awe. She was there just for the summer. "You are so brave." I commented. "No" she said in very broken English, "I came here with my classmate." "How many?" I asked. "One," she answered. Wherever we went the name tags told us where the seasonal employees were from. They were from faraway places like China, Ecuador, Russia, and they were also from different parts of the United States. I wanted to know if they were enjoying their experience and almost all of them told me they were having a wonderful time. One young woman said she couldn't believe someone was paying her to show people the beauty of Yellowstone. This same young woman had spent a few of her free days hiking and tenting in the park with another gal, just them and their bear spray! Another young man said it was his fourth summer. "What's not to like? I'm getting paid and in my free time I get to hike and fish."

When my husband and I talk about the opportunities presented to us as young people, we recognize that we simply had no knowledge of the kind of experiences that might have been available then and that are available to people today.

We met some of the coolest adults while traveling through the National Parks. It was the fourteenth year of service for one of the seasonal rangers we met. For me the most fascinating thing is everyone with whom I spoke was having a wonderful time. Did you know people of all ages can work as seasonal workers in the parks? The first time I met an older adult who worked in the parks was in Yosemite. Sandy and I went to a Sunday service in the tiny church in the park. At one point we were encouraged to greet the other people attending the service and to chat with each other. One woman we greeted told us she and her husband were seasonal workers. They had sold their home and all of its contents, bought an RV and each year since, they had chosen a different park to work in during the summer. My eyes were as big as quarters as I listened. My husband looked shocked. I think he was afraid I was going to head home and begin the process of becoming a National Park gypsy.

One of our guides, Keith Watts with Earth Tours, shared with us the story of how he met his wife. It was July in Alaska and he was doing research, out in the wild all by himself. He was a professor of geology at one of the universities, and in the summers he trekked through the wilderness for weeks on end collecting samples. One evening the weather turned unusually cold and it began to snow. He was concerned about getting back to civilization when he heard voices off in the distance. He could see through his binoculars that three people were huddled around a fire with a raft pulled up onto the shore. As he was looking through his binoculars, one of the women on the river trip was looking through her binoculars; their eyes met and it was love at first sight. They had been married 14 years at the time of his story. He said his friends were right when they told him it would be "a snowy day in July" before he met someone who would marry him. He went onto say she saved him in more ways than one. He wasn't sure he would have made it out of the wilderness if he hadn't met up with them and their raft. His wife-to-be and two friends had been dropped off at the top of a seldom-traveled river with a pickup date and time, scheduled for two weeks later. It was quite a daring thing to do but it wasn't her first trek into the unknown. As a young single mother she had gone to live with friends, saved all her money, and had taken her 12-year-old son on a two-year trek around the world in a van.

"Who are these people?" It's all I can think to ask when I meet these adventurous spirits. It's all I can think to ask when I read and hear about the pioneers of the past. I believe there's a fine line between bravery and stupidity. Sometimes I think the only way to know which side of the line one is on, is afterwards, by the results of one's actions. If you enter into a dangerous situation and you come through unscathed or stronger for it, you might be considered brave. If you don't come through, you'll probably be considered stupid but don't all pioneers begin their journeys on paths unknown and untested? Where would we be without people willing to step way outside of their comfort zones?

In the Grand Tetons, we also had the opportunity to watch several para-gliders come off one of the mountains and soar above us as they came to land at our feet. It was mesmerizing to watch. I was ready to give it a try but I wondered, "Who are these people?" Who was the first one to step off the mountain with a parachute attached to them? Were they brave or were they stupid? Does it matter? If no one is willing to go out and see and try that which is new, there would be no growth. Think of all we would be missing today!

I, for one, am grateful for the spirit that takes people to places unknown. I am grateful for those in our society willing to challenge themselves so that those of us who are not as adventurous or as spirited get to follow in their footsteps. We get to see, enjoy and experience things we might never have had the opportunity to experience except that they paved the way for us. They are our forefathers and our foremothers and they are those who are still with us, the students and seasonal workers of our parks and perhaps those amazing people within our circles who also help us broaden our horizons because of their bravery and courage.

For me this is the blessing of travel. I get to see the world differently than I would have had I stayed home in my cozy little world. I meet people I'd never have otherwise met and hear stories I'd never have heard if I were afraid to venture outside of my comfort zone. It's true, I wasn't the first to step off the mountain and try to soar; I am not the one living in a tent and listening for bears; I'm not the one rafting down an unknown river or even taking a new job in an unfamiliar location, but I am the one enjoying the fruits of all these pioneers because I am the one, perhaps a lot like you, that did travel to unknown places both out in the world and then, even more importantly, inside to within to my heart and spirit. Discovering at least a few times in my life when I could answer, "I am one of those people."

Who Would You Die For?

Affirmation: *I recognize and fully appreciate who and what are important to me in my life.*

I read a news article about Greg Gadson, a lieutenant colonel with the Second Battalion and 32nd Field Artillery. He was stationed in Baghdad when his vehicle hit a roadside bomb. He remembered being placed on a stretcher with his severed feet in his lap. The next time he was conscious both his legs had been amputated above the knees. The picture in the paper showed a broad-shouldered, strong-looking man with two artificial legs, wearing shorts. The story went on to say that he had recently been given a role in the movie *Battleship*. His inspirational journey to healing had brought him fame but his journey wasn't just focused on himself. He had a message, a mission statement, that he had developed through his challenge back to wholeness and he was sharing it with other service members. His message was "Whenever you have a formidable task, instead of looking up, look down. Literally take it one step at a time. You'll be overwhelmed by the broader view." I was inspired but I was also surprised by this statement. It seemed to me that he would be very hesitant to look down. The article went on to say that this amazing man didn't show one ounce of self pity.

I've often wondered how I would respond and who I would be in times of great challenge?" I've always wanted to believe I'd be a heroine, acting honorably and bravely. Certainly I've had challenges in my life and mostly I've responded with courage and integrity, but when I read stories about people like Greg Gadson, I find myself wondering, "What if that happened to me?" There are so many tales of amazing people who have made extraordinary efforts to help others at a great cost to themselves and it has cost some their lives. These people are not all past heroes. There are many with us today and there is so much to be learned from them.

In Small Christian Community, a study group at church my husband and I have been with since 1987, we often discuss the great sacrifice made by Jesus Christ to lead us to a different, broader, and more loving perception of God the Father. Often, the question arises "Who would you die for?" I find myself thinking about all our soldiers who have given their lives for us and in most cases, we are total strangers.

My oldest daughter, Melissa, is an amazing mother. She's exceptionally young looking. She's always looked much younger than her years.[7] She was engaged when she was in her early 20s, and one day we went to the local department store to shop for a few wedding accessories. The saleswoman was shocked when we told her we were there for my daughter's wedding. She said to my daughter in an indignant tone, "How old are you?" I smiled because I knew she was going to be amazed by the answer; in fact I'm not sure she even believed us. The reason I'm sharing this story is because when my granddaughter, Isabelle, started school, the teacher took a very superior attitude toward my daughter. The teacher really thought my daughter was a child raising a child, but my daughter was older than she realized, and much, much wiser than she the teacher ever imagined. When it comes to her children, my daughter is like a mother bear. You do not want to mess with her and I'm really proud of her for that. Not that she dismisses the concerns of the teachers, but she carefully examines their reactions to her children and demands a nonpartisan, professional attitude from them, as she should. I mention this because most mothers will do whatever it takes to protect their children.

I took a one-night self-defense class many years ago and was instructed to "bite the nose off" of my attacker. All the women in the class moaned in disgust. Then the instructor said, "Make believe he's attacking your daughter." The entire atmosphere changed. There was not one woman there who wasn't ready to do whatever it took to make sure their child was safe. I've never watched the movie *Sophie's Choice*. I know the premise of the story was she had to choose who of her children

---

[7] I like to think she got that quality from me!

would live and who would die. I can't even imagine such a situation and I don't want to watch someone have to make such a decision but many people are faced with impossible decisions, many of which I hope I'm never faced.

The question not only revolves around who, but what: "What would you die for?" "What do you hold so precious that you would give up your life?" The young men and women who serve in our armed forces hold our way of life here in America so precious that they are willing to die for it. I don't fully agree with all of the wars in which America has chosen to participate. I'm not sure how I would have responded to being drafted to fight in Vietnam. It was one more decision I wasn't faced with making but we have lost so many very young men and women to conflicts. It's heartbreaking.

I was sitting in a waiting room at UNC hospital one day when a young man in uniform walked in. I watched in awe and with a sense of shame as one of the other women who was also waiting, got up and went over to the soldier and simply said, "Thank you." Thank you! I found it to be such a powerful gesture. I haven't let a soldier pass me by since then without stopping them and saying, "Thank you."

What is the message here? All of us have something or someone we are willing to die for. All of us have something or someone we are willing to live for. It's important to know and to take the time to recognize what's important to you. It's nice to have the luxury of not being in a horrible situation before you find out what or who they are. Think about it and maybe you'll be able to fully recognize and appreciate who and what are of the greatest importance in your life and be grateful while you still have the time to say, "Thank you."

An Unexpected Life

Affirmation: *I let go of regret.*

What did you dream your life would be like? Do you still have dreams and expectations about how your life will be in the future? It seems there's been so much written about "bucket lists," things people always wanted to do but never got around to and so they are making an extra effort to do it now before it's too late. There's been a movie by that title and there's a country-western song about it, too. I certainly have a list. Mostly it involves places I'd like to see before I die. My husband, Sandy, bought me a book called *A Thousand Places to See Before You Die*. I immediately started going through it to see where I had not been. He was looking at it, too, but he was noting all the places we'd already been, two very different perspectives.

According to the Enneagram Personality System, I am a type 7: I am always looking for the next experience, the next adventure. This type is not easily contented. I am always on the lookout for what I might have missed. In some ways it makes life exciting, but in other ways it can prevent me from relishing the present since I'm always looking forward. For me, dreaming and planning for the future lead me to feeling optimistic. I like believing there will be a future to plan for but I believe it's also important to let go of things we imagined might have been.

I once mentioned to a friend that as a young woman I had dreamed of living and working in Manhattan. She told me it was never too late to pursue a dream. I believe that but I think sometimes it's better to let go of some dreams. I expected to graduate from college and head off to New York City. I didn't dream of being on Broadway. I dreamed of being on Wall Street. My life, however, took me in another direction. I made decisions that led me to suburbia and even further out into rural

America. I've lived in several states but I've never lived in "the city." Sometimes I found myself fantasizing about the life I had dreamed about. It was very different from the life I had. Boy, I am good at imagining all the wonderful experiences and adventures I would have had.

I attended a retreat once with a woman who had six children. She also had a sister who had become a cloistered nun. She told us she was much younger than her sister and was very confused and saddened by her sister's choice. She said she could only go visit her sister once a year, and it was so quiet and it seemed so lonely. Then, she shared that after being married for twenty years and raising six children, she'd had many moments when she wished she'd joined the convent. I know she was teasing us but there was also an element of truth in her statement. The story in the cartoon *UP* revolves around a married couple who had a dream about moving to an exotic country and living above the waterfalls. Every year they saved for their travel and every year something came along that derailed their adventure. When the wife dies, the man, who at this point is quite elderly and very depressed, decides it's finally time to give it a go. He attaches hundreds of balloons to the top of his house and he floats away to find the waterfalls. Once again, he's derailed but this time he has a new friend, a young boy who has hidden away in his house, who helps him see the world differently. In looking over his wife's "dream journal," he realizes she had added pictures to the album that had nothing to do with their ultimate goal of moving to the exotic location: she added pictures of their life together, of the adventure they'd actually had during their life's journey.

There's a study that shows people age better when they can let go of regret. Carol Klein addressed this issue in her book *Overcoming Regret*. What happens when we cling to regret is that we idealize a situation that may have turned out completely different from our imagination. Once we realize that we don't have a clue how something would have turned out, perhaps if we could even imagine how horrible it might have been rather than some fantasy we've been clinging to, maybe then we can let go of that regret and fully appreciate the life we have.

The title of Queen Noor's memoir, *A Leap of Faith, Memories of an Unexpected Life*, made me think. I wondered when I saw that title how many people have lived an expected life. I took a small survey and asked several friends if they'd lived an "expected life." I only had one person say yes. What is your answer? I can tell you right now I never dreamed of the life I've lived and am now living. Never, never did I imagine myself living in North Carolina surrounded by my family. I never thought I'd travel to China or Ecuador or some of the other amazing places I've been. My life has been a series of adventures and mysteries and it's been great! Once I was able to let go of the "what might have been," like the man in *UP*, I was able to appreciate what has been.

Perhaps the secret is not to let go of our dreams or our "bucket lists," but to let go of expecting life to be exactly as we imagined and to embrace it as it is, to relish all we have experienced, all we have learned.

Perhaps the secret is to treasure whatever life has afforded us, the expected and the unexpected.

Perception

Affirmation: *I am the product of my genes and my thoughts and my thoughts influence my cellular structure.*

Stephen Covey, author of the *7 Habits of Highly Effective People*, tells a story about a man on a subway train with his children. The children are out of control and most of the people on the train are looking very annoyed. Have you ever ridden the subway? Usually the only noise one hears is the train itself. It can be a very meditative space. Finally the man looks up and explains to the people in his immediate area that his wife has just died and he's not sure what to do next. No one was annoyed any longer. They shifted their perception but the question that comes to my mind is: Couldn't they have held a more compassionate response to the family without that information? If they were going to judge, couldn't they have given him, the father, the benefit of the doubt in the beginning?

I play the fiddle. I seldom claim to be a fiddler. It's the same with golf. I usually say, "I play golf." I have never said, "I am a golfer." Can you hear the difference? There are titles I claim for myself but fiddler and golfer are neither of them.

I began receiving a message about perception in many of my conversations and in several of my readings. I considered how we perceive (judge) what others "do" or "don't do" and how we relate their behavior to ourselves. I believe we sometimes perceive ourselves through the behavior of another.

I like for people to be happy. I like them to feel good. I can sometimes try to orchestrate another's feel-good mood even if I don't really know them very well. I will normally remove myself from someone who is grouchy and complaining. I am compassionate and I have learned you don't always need to comfort people in pain; sometimes you need to simply sit with them and allow them to experience their feelings. I encourage smiles and warm hearts. I find it quite easy to raise people's spirits with a smile, a hug, or a genuine warm welcome. Usually people respond in a very positive manner.

What about those who do not respond? Am I the reason? Did I do or not do something? Is everyone's happiness my responsibility? Sister Mary Margaret from A Place for Women to Gather says, "Happiness is an inside job." There is only one person's happiness and sense of well-being I am responsible for, mine. I'd like to believe I am all powerful and can influence the emotional state of everyone in my life but I can't. Truth to tell whether they are happy or unhappy usually has very little, if anything, to do with me. It's all about them. Then there's all that stuff we make up in our minds about what people are thinking, and there's the rub.

My plan for playing the fiddle at my group's very first performance was to occasionally fake fiddle. There were twelve of us; who, other than my teacher, could possibly tell if I missed a few notes or dropped out if I were totally lost? Well, the two people who sat down only four feet from me were concert musicians. I had recently been introduced to them and I was told the gentleman was a concert violinist and composer and he was directly in front of me! I knew without a doubt that they could hear every wrong note I hit and I hit many, many wrong notes. I knew what they were thinking. I made up a whole story in my head and it wasn't very affirming. In fact, it was quite demoralizing.

No, I couldn't stop and turn my thinking around. There was just too much going on for me to calm myself. The day after the recital, however, I realized what I had done. I had robbed myself of the joy of the moment by imagining the thoughts of two people I didn't even know. And even if they thought my fiddling was substandard, why should I care? I was with my friends, making music and playing for free for the benefit of others. Oh, it's not the first time I've compared my inside with someone else's outside and every time it's a devaluing experience. But, each time I do it, I become more aware of the exercise and hopefully recognize my behavior and let go of what I think they're thinking and let go of caring what the other person or persons are thinking. "Happiness is an inside job," and I can choose for myself not to be reactive to my imagination. Or, I can choose to imagine with compassion and kindness whether I'm imagining for myself or about others.

Our life is our perception. Choose carefully. Be kind to yourself and to those around you.

The Big Picture

Affirmation: *Because of my relationship with my Lord Jesus Christ, I let go of fear and anxiety and fully trust in His loving care for me.*

Have you heard the story about the farmer who lived in ancient times who had a lovely farm, one son, and one horse? One day the farmer and his son found the gate to the corral open and the horse missing. All his friends and neighbors gathered around and said, "Oh no, you poor man. You've lost your only horse; how terrible!" He answered, "Maybe yes, maybe no." His son then borrowed a horse and went to look for their missing animal. In a while, his father looked up and saw his son coming toward him riding the missing horse and behind him was an entire herd of horses. He opened the gate and all the horses ran into the corral. All his friends and neighbors gathered around and said, "Oh, you lucky man. You've not only found your horse. You now have a whole herd of horses; how wonderful!" He answered, "Maybe yes, maybe no." His son began taming the wild horses, but one day he fell off and broke his leg. All his friends and neighbors gathered around and said, "Oh no, you poor man. Your only son has broken his leg and now he cannot help you with all the work on your farm; how terrible!" He answered, "Maybe yes, maybe no." While his son was recuperating, the local warlord and his men showed up. They were conscripting all eligible young men to fight in their war. Of course, they could not take the farmer's son because of his broken leg. Once again, all his friends and neighbors gathered around and said, "Oh, you lucky man. Your only son has been saved from fighting for the local warlord; how wonderful!" I'm not going to tell you his answer. I think you already know it.

How many times have you had something happen and you judged the quality of the experience as good or bad, but then later (sometimes much later) saw it in a different light and realized you didn't have a clue at the time it occurred about how it was going to affect your life? It's so easy to fall into the pit of despair, anxiety, and depression. According to quantum physics, negative energy resonates at a lower level than positive energy. That makes it easier for us to connect with it and more difficult to tap into the positive. We have to work harder to find the positive. I'm sure you have many examples of events that created openings into opportunities of which you never dreamed. In our family alone, we have experienced job loss that led to a new and better opportunity. We've witnessed the sad dissolution of a marriage that later led to a new, healthier, happier family unit. We've seen so much suffering and struggle that in time brought reward and accomplishment. Of course that's not always true but it can bring comfort that it could work out for the better.

That's not to say we shouldn't allow ourselves our feelings. Not only should we allow them, we need to experience them. There is no shortcut through grief; there is only the direct path through it. If you try to skirt around it, it will catch up with you when you least expect it. Grief can come from many different types of losses, not just from death. One can experience grief over the loss of a dream; perhaps the dream of a perfect marriage, a perfect job, the dream of what one thought a perfect career should look like. One can experience grief over the loss of health, money, youth, and even less-recognized events like that of thinning hair or a thickening middle. It's all part of our lives. It's important to acknowledge how we feel about loss and then move towards recovery. It's also important to realize nothing is stagnant. Life is always changing and whatever is causing you distress will change too and it might just be the one thing to open a door to something marvelous. Why not simply watch and see how it works itself out?

We are only capable of seeing a small part of the picture. Only God can see the big picture. The question is, can you trust enough to believe He/She has your best interest at heart, and that thing which was meant for your harm, God will use for your good? Garth Brooks has a song entitled "Thank God for Unanswered Prayer." In it he tells the story of a man who meets an old flame, the one woman he prayed to God to make his wife. It didn't work out and now as he walks away from her, he realizes how lucky he was. He's married to the real love of his life and so he remembers to "thank God for unanswered prayer." It's another example of loss and grief and an experience that led to something better. I'm sure he couldn't see it when it happened. He had to wait to recognize the blessing that came from the breakup with his first love.

For me, this is why I practice my faith. I don't want it to be all about life after death. I want to live this life with the trust that God really does want only my best and that if I practice that, if I trust, all will be well. It may not be the way I expected. It may not be anything like what I had asked for but, if I believe that whatever is happening is exactly what should be happening, think of the peace I experience. I must confess it's not an easy process, simple maybe, but not easy. It takes work. It takes staying connected to the Divine at every possible moment. I have a wonderful CD, *Meditation to Help You with Chemotherapy*, by Belleruth Naparstak. At one point in the tape she speaks about all the angels and guides who are surrounding the listener and then as they begin to fade away they say, "Remember, we are always with you. It is you who comes and goes." What comfort that brings me. If I can stay focused, if I choose to stay in the presence of God, God will always be with me. That's my choice; that's my meditation; to remain in the presence of God and with all my angels and helpers as often as possible and to trust in their divine protection. Then, when faced with a challenging situation instead of labeling it "good or bad, lucky or unlucky," I can simply watch it and think, "maybe yes, maybe no."

Faith or Fear? You Choose

Affirmation: *I choose Faith over fear.*

The paper the technician handed me read, "We are pleased to inform you that the results of your recent mammogram show no evidence of cancer." I had dodged another bullet. I had escaped death once again. I could breathe a little easier for another year. It had been over a decade since I was treated for cancer but somehow it didn't matter on the morning I had my appointment. It's usually a very early appointment. I have an hour's drive and I have trouble getting out of the house. I know why. I have the same trouble getting to the dentist on time. I was afraid. I was nervous. Mind you, I am not planning on getting cancer again (of course, I wasn't planning on getting it the first time). I know a lot of people who carry around the worry of a cancer diagnosis, especially if there's a family history. My elderly aunt had breast cancer and my father died of a brain tumor at the age of 62, but I have taken really good care of myself. I eat right, I exercise and I monitor my thoughts. I never dreamed I'd have breast cancer. I was truly shocked when I was given the diagnosis.

I have since discovered it's not an unusual reaction. Many people are simply rolling along when they receive this diagnosis. The truth is we should be less surprised to not receive some sort of health challenge at some point in our lives rather than the other way around. One man who is a patient at the Preston Robert Tisch Brain Tumor Center told a group of us that he had a headache and surprisingly woke up from it in the hospital. He was a very robust man with an abundant amount of energy and a big personality. He heard them saying, "You have a brain tumor, a glioblastoma." He laughed and said, "You're talking to the wrong person. You've made a mistake." But they hadn't.

These diagnoses are like terrorist attacks. One day you're walking down the street and boom, a bomb goes off. There might have been a warning sign but many times there is not. One of my physicians graciously told me that the cancer wasn't anything I did or didn't do; it was a "random act of violence." In one way, that gave me a lot of comfort. I didn't need to find blame either within or without but it meant that I was vulnerable to the whims of the world and with that thought, I found I felt unsafe. It left me fearful. I wondered what else was going on inside my body that I was totally unaware of and I was afraid.

Fear can be a debilitating disease. It can rob us of our joy, of some of our happiest moments. It can steal our whole lives from us if we let it but how do we deal with it? When I was invited to join my daughter-in-law on a trip to Ecuador, I didn't hesitate to say yes, but I want to confess: I was afraid. I have read many stories of people being abducted in third-world counties and taken off into the jungle, or worse and being held for years and years. I knew this fear of being kidnapped was irrational, but was it? Maybe I simply wasn't listening to my spiritual guides who were telling me not to go? But I wasn't going to miss this opportunity so my guides and angels had better step up and protect me. I was also extra vigilant and extremely careful. As I sat on the steps of the Virgin de Panecillo at the top of Quito looking out over the evening lights of the whole city, I cried. I thought, "Fear might have kept me from having this experience. How horrible that would have been." It wasn't the first time I shed tears on that trip and it wasn't the last. It was an amazing journey.

So, on that early Friday morning when I was heading off for my yearly mammogram, I recognized the visitor who had arrived with the ringing of my alarm clock. Fear was here. I recall the first time I heard the phrase "Faith or fear." It was in a sermon at a church I was visiting in Arizona. It was one of those moments when I felt a light go on. I knew exactly what the priest was talking about. I had a choice. How was I going to live my life? I decided right then and there I was not going to have my life's choices dictated by fear. And, I have been deciding that every day ever since. I have had to make it a meditation. There are days, like on that early Friday morning of my appointment, when I had to decide moment to moment to stay centered and calm. Deciding was the easy part; making the choice, putting it into practice, well, that's a whole other story. Once again, I was faced with finding a way to live with Faith and to let go of the fear. That's when I created the affirmation, *"I choose Faith over fear."* It's evolved over the years. I now focus not only on letting go of those emotions that don't serve me but also on strengthening my faith. I have several affirmations that I say to increase my sense of well-being; to make me believe that no matter what is happening, I am all right because my faith is strong and helping me to stay in a good place.

I am now officially a "cancer survivor." You actually get to claim that title whenever you want. There are no hard and fast rules. A few years back my breast oncologist approached me with the concept of creating a Survivorship Clinic, where women like myself, women who were out of treatment for several years and appear to be doing well, would visit for their yearly appointment instead of seeing him. I agreed. My visit at Duke this Friday morning was to be in this clinic with a nursing assistant who specialized in breast cancer treatment. It included an hour group session, the mammogram, and a full exam. Well, I really didn't need a group session. There wasn't really any more information I could gather. I was fine, right?

There I sat with six other people, only three patients, a nutritionist, a breast oncologist and the NA. The topics quickly turned to how to stay optimally healthy, what effect a breast cancer diagnosis and treatment has on long-term health, and what our best choices might be. It was a delightful morning, informative and empowering. The other people in the group were very interesting. The information they shared was extremely helpful. I invited a dear friend to join me for the mammogram appointment. We had a nice visit—actually, I had a really good time. I was given that wonderful paper announcing my cancer-free breasts, I learned some new things, I had a wonderful exam, I visited with a dear friend, and I met a few new really interesting people.

I made it back from Ecuador without being kidnapped. I made it through my yearly breast appointment without a cancer diagnosis. I know I will experience other challenges in my life, things I may not even be able to imagine but with my focus on faith, by letting go of the fear, I hope that whatever life brings, I will have at some point in the experience tears of joy and be saying to myself, "Fear might have kept me from having this experience. How horrible that would have been."

Loving Speech

Affirmation: *I am committed to cultivating loving speech and deep listening.*

What do you like to talk about? What topics make you sit up and get interested in the conversation? I remember the first time I heard the phrase, "If you don't have anything nice to say, come sit here by me." It was in the movie *Steel Magnolias*, spoken by Olympia Dukakis. It's a paraphrase of a famous quote from Alice Roosevelt Longworth: "If you haven't got anything nice to say about anybody, come sit next to me." All I can say about that is, I hope I'm remembered for saying something more along the lines of John Lennon ("Give Peace a Chance") or the above affirmation, "***I am committed to cultivating loving speech and deep listening***," taken from Buddhist monk Thich Nhat Hanh's *Coming Home*.

When I heard those words in *Steel Magnolias* I was shocked. I was so surprised that someone so openly relished talking badly about another. I think most of the people in my life make an effort to be kind to and about one another. Sure, there's the occasional slip but I don't have a lot of people in my life who talk maliciously about others. I must confess that I can be guilty about getting caught up in a conversation when it becomes "gossipy." I can be very curious about what they have to say and there have been times in my life when I have had a tough time with someone and felt a desperate need to share the experience with another, all from my slanted point of view.

Is it all right to talk about others? Do you think it's OK to tell tales about people? When you begin talking about another person is there a way to do it with love and kindness even when he or she has injured you? When I am wounded or slighted, I usually seek support from loved ones by telling my story. It's not usually just the facts. It's usually about my emotional reactions. Most of us need to seek comfort from others when we have a difficult experience. We need to tell our story but we get to choose how we tell it. Do we tear down and berate the other or do we do it with kindness and gentleness, even toward our enemies?

I am very judgmental about judgmental people. When someone in my life has a tendency to label people as "good or bad," "nice or mean," or as "someone they like a lot," which means there are others that they don't like at all, I find myself recoiling from them. If they judge everyone else, they must have a very definitive opinion about me and I become very leery.

Many years ago I hired a young person to help me do some painting around the house. In the process I needed to empty out my closet and I was somewhat embarrassed by the number of shoes I owned. I mentioned it to him adding an apology and he stopped me before I even got all the words out. He then declared, "I'm not here to judge anyone." I'm not here to judge anyone! Yes, I would like to claim that as a character trait. I do affirm *"I love unconditionally, non-judgmentally and non-graspingly."* It's an intention I've set for those who are close to me in my life but when it comes to the rest of the world, can I be non-judgmental? Probably not but I can try. The truth is that I seldom have the whole picture. I only have that little piece that I can see.

The gym I've always belonged to has a large senior population. Once when I was there, there was a new plaque on an easel and I stopped to check it out. It was a photo of a plane from WWII with a huge hole in the right wing. Framed with it was a thank you from one of the members, Hal Shook, for the service of the people who work at our gym and an award, The Legion of Honor, that he received in 2011 (more than 60 years after the end of the war). After I viewed the framed presentation, I found myself wondering about all those people I usually see there. I began to wonder about what I've been missing by not getting to know some of these individuals. I am sure this gentleman is not the only hero who is walking around that gym. I wondered if I were to see him what sort of judgment would I form? Would I have guessed his honorary past? Why then should I judge at all? My job is simply to observe.

In Kripalu Yoga we incorporate BRFWA into our yoga practice, which means, "breathe, relax, feel, watch, and allow." Nowhere does it tell me I need to judge my practice or myself. We are also instructed to not make yoga into a completive sport. "Stay on your mat; don't go invading someone else's practice, watching them, and comparing yourself to them." These are the same lessons we can take with us into the world. I actually think the affirmation should be, "I am committed to cultivating loving <u>thoughts</u> and deep listening." Maybe if I worked on that regularly, the loving speech would simply become second nature.

The Third Klesha, Attachment

Affirmation: *I love unconditionally, non-judgmentally and without attachment.*

At the church service I attended, the homily cited the New Testament Book of John 12:20–33, which says, "Whoever loves his life loses it, and whoever hates his life in this world will preserve it for eternal life." I must say I was a little worried by this scripture. I love my life. Does that mean I am destined to eternal Hell? I've worked really hard to reach a place where I can claim that I love my life. According to the priest, however, I was in deep trouble. I really wanted to put my hand up and say, "Father, I don't believe that. Can we discuss this a little further? I have a few ideas and I'd like to open this whole concept up for more discussion." Unfortunately, or perhaps fortunately, that is not an option that I've ever seen happen in the middle of mass. Oh, I've seen people get up and walk out when they disagreed with what was being said, but I've never (and I've been going to church for well over half a century) seen anyone ask for clarification during a sermon. That did, however, give me the opportunity to examine this closer and to examine what I think Christ was telling us. Most of His message is about one thing: Love. So, how would this scripture be interpreted in the light of love?

Have you noticed that we are creatures of habit? Speaking of church, have you noticed that people always tend to sit in the same section, some in the same pew, and others only in one specific seat? In church someone sat behind me one day and I heard her say in exasperation, "Someone is in my seat." Now, I'm not familiar with all the places of worship in the world, but in the churches and synagogues I've been in, I've never seen a nameplate on the seat of a bench. I am fascinated by this desire for certainty.

The gym I belong to has several types of fitness classes and people there also seem to need to be in the same place every time they attend a class. One day I watched a gentleman set up his equipment in an area he wasn't aware "belonged" to another lady. She came into the class and went over to him to tell him he was in her spot. I was dumbfounded (and I must confess I judged her harshly even though it had nothing to do with me). I was curious how this interaction would go and was charmed when the usurper apologized for not paying closer attention, thanked her for informing him, and picked up his stuff and moved over. I've also been in a similar situation in a dance class and couldn't figure out why this woman who came in late kept stepping on my toes as we bounced across the gym floor until I finally realized, I was in her spot.

My main concern with this type of attachment is for my own well-being. I'm afraid if I stay in the same place whenever I'm in a familiar locale my mind will stop expanding, my neurotransmitters will get smaller and smaller, and so will my whole world. I know the importance of stepping outside of my comfort zone. If I'm aware of my desire for routine, even small ones, like eating at the same place in the kitchen every morning, or choosing the same food for lunch every day, and choose differently on occasion, I know that adjusting to larger challenges will be easier and not only will my mind not shrink but my world won't shrink. I don't want to live in a small world; I'm all into keeping "green."

There is a tale about a Buddhist monk who was being threatened by a civilian soldier. The soldier shouted at him, "Don't you know who I am? Don't you know I can take your life?" The monk looked at him calmly and said, "Don't you know who I am? Don't you know that I don't care?" and then the monk slowly walked away. That is not being attached.

Patanjali, the "Grandfather of Yoga," claimed that by practicing the eight limbs of yoga one would be helped with conquering the five human afflictions, or *kleshas*, that cause suffering: ignorance, egoism, attachment, aversion and possessiveness. The third klesha, attachment (or *raga*), creates in us a pattern of acquisition: we began to pursue human relationships, knowledge, wealth, status, power—anything that might be capable of enlarging and protecting our fragile individualized existence. But because change is the nature of creation all objects within it are impermanent, and thus subject to loss at any moment.[8]

In the March 1993 issue of *Guideposts* magazine there was a short article by Catherine Marshall called "Prayer of Relinquishment." In it, she told the story of Mrs. Nathaniel Hawthorne, wife of the famous American author. In 1860, Mrs. Hawthorne was in Rome, immersed in prayer. Their oldest daughter Una was dying. As she urgently prayed for their daughter's healing, a strange thought arose in her: She decided to let Una go. She prayed to God to take Una, if that was best. "I give her to Him. No, I won't fight against Him anymore." According to the story, an even stranger thing then happened. Minutes later Mrs. Hawthorne returned to their daughter's bedside and found the girl sleeping naturally, without temperature or restlessness. She was healed.

When I begin my yoga practice, I do three Sun Salutations. In the first one I thank God, out loud, "for the beautiful new day" and as I reach for the ground in a standing forward bend (*uttanasana*), I say, "and I relinquish it to You." In the second one, I thank God for "this amazing life and I relinquish it to You" and in the third Salutation I pray, "Thank You, Lord Jesus for this amazing, healthy, healing body and I relinquish it to You." Oh, yes, I take it back over and over during the day but each morning I begin anew.

This is the message I believe Christ was sharing with us. We must die to self and relinquish attachment. We must let go of all the stuff that we think we possess because in reality it possesses us. We are being called upon to believe in the goodness and ultimate care of a loving God, someone whom we can trust will care for all of our needs. We don't need to be in charge. We don't need to hold on tight. We are being called upon to recognize that everything in our life, except God, is temporary and we are being told that when we can recognize and accept that principle, life will be more meaningful; we will be lighter and freer.

---

[8] Sarasvati Buhrman: "Leaving Depression Behind-the Yogic Way Out." *Yoga International*, February/March 27, 1998. Accessed 2013, http://www.physics.udel.edu/~bnikolic/klesa.html

Younger Next Year

Affirmation: *Healing is within my power.*

What age would you tell someone you are if you didn't know what age you are? Stephen Levine asked this question at a seminar on death and dying many years ago. Sometimes I find myself asking myself that question. When I'm on a golf course, I feel about 25, not because I'm a good golfer but because I always feel like a newbie even though I have played on and off for over 40 years. After I was treated for cancer, I felt like I aged about ten years in a single year: Before cancer I would have answered that I was about 35; after cancer I felt like 45 (I guess that was OK since at the time I was treated, I was 52).

Over a decade ago I first visited Canyon Ranch in Arizona. I was looking for a way to learn about how to best take care of my health; I had read a lot about the resort and decided to give it a try. It's a wonderful place, very holistic and almost surreal. It met all my expectations. While I was there, the founder and owner, Mel Zuckerman, offered an early morning presentation about the beginning of the ranch and why he started it. He was very dynamic and I found his story to be quite inspirational. He said when he first arrived in Arizona he was not in good health. One of the first tests he took determined his "age" based on his physical condition. He was about 55 at the time and the test came back that he was in his 70s. At the time of his presentation, he actually was in his 70s and after years of training and healthy food and other practices, his "age" tested at 55. Back then that seemed like a radical concept, becoming younger as one ages, but now there is a lot of information about getting stronger and healthier as we age. One of my personal favorites is *Younger Next Year* by Chris Crowley and Henry S. Lodge, M.D.

A friend once told me, "Growing old is not for the weak of heart." I know the number one determining factor about how (and if) we age is purely genetic. The second most influential factor is how and what we think about the aging process. At the Omega Institute's first Conscious Aging Conference, one speaker shared his research into the number one factor concerning the age at which we will die, which was determined mostly by when we thought we would die.

As the time of this writing my mother's best friend is 99. Many mornings when I am entering the gym at 9:00 a.m. or 9:30 a.m. she is on her way out. She has already finished her workout. She pedals the bike for 15 minutes, she uses the rowing machine for 15 minutes, and then she does the weight machine circuit. She drove herself there until she was 97. Afterward, she heads to Trader Joe's for her daily shopping expedition. She is one of my heroines. She had a broken tibia when she was 94 and was in rehab for almost nine months. I was sure that was "it" for her as I couldn't imagine her recovering from such a break at such an advanced age. It's good I didn't share that with her because she never doubted she was going to heal and return to living in her own home on her own and back to a full, rich life … and so she did!

Have you listened to what people say about their health? Have you had the opportunity to hear people speak about their memory loss, their back pain, their bum knees, dimming eyesight, etc.? It seems a day never passes when someone isn't claiming that age is the reason for some ailment with which they are dealing. People seem to be looking for a reason why they are deteriorating and it's so easy to claim it's related to physical age.

In Dr. Andrew Weil's PBS special on how to live a healthier older life, he recognized that the body does change, and that we might need to make adjustments as we go along. Most of us seem to fall into that category, and then there are the people who are in their 80s or 90s and are still running marathons. What works for one simply may not work for another. We need to create a personal life plan for each individual.

My cousin's mother was almost 100 when she was diagnosed with dementia. Of course, they were told, it was a normal condition for someone her age. Another physician asked the family if their mother had been tested for a thyroid problem. No, she had not been tested. A few days after beginning the proper medication, she was back to her normal self.

Do yourself a favor: Don't claim your ailments. Certainly, they can be a part of your life but let them be just that: a part of your life. Don't let them determine who you are. Don't identify with them. Even a serious diagnosis does not have to determine your identity. I have met more people who introduce themselves to me by telling me about their physical challenges. Sometimes, it's the first thing they tell me after their name. I want to shout, "Get behind me Satan! Don't do that! You are greater than whatever ailment you're dealing with. Find another way to view yourself, to view your problem." Truly, it's not a lack of compassion on my part. It's actually very compassionate. I want to tell them they are injuring themselves even further by focusing on their diagnosis. Put it aside, put it on a shelf, and go do something fun or better yet, go do something for someone else.

You have the power to heal yourself! It is within all of us. Claim it! Yes, it may mean making some changes, getting help. It may mean medication, surgery, or a change in diet and exercise, but listen closely and you will know what you need to do to help yourself. But the first thing you need to do is to not identify with your diagnosis. You need to find a way to make peace, to just allow it to be and to move away and forward. You've seen and met people who not only refuse to allow their ailments and disabilities to interfere with their lives, but who thrive in spite of them. It is possible for all of us. What do you think the Olympic athletes tell themselves? Do you think they focus on their aches, pains, or ailments? I doubt it.

Rachel Naomi Remen, in *Kitchen Table Wisdom*, speaks about healing. She says that sometimes we will not be cured but we can always be healed. What we think about, we bring about. You might be dealing with a serious illness but if you choose your thoughts carefully you will recognize that you are a glorious creature of God. You are beautiful! You are amazing! You still have a life to live and love to bestow! We need to hold onto the belief that the best is yet to come and that we get to choose whether or not to believe it, and whether or not we will create it.

How powerful is that? We get to choose. We decide day to day, moment to moment, how we perceive ourselves; how we perceive our abilities; how we perceive our bodies. It's our greatest power. It's the one thing we have total (at most times) control over. Claim your health! Claim your strength! Whatever it is that is interfering with your optimal health needs to be reframed, adjusted. You may not be training for the Olympics, but you will still benefit from a new thought process that will enable you to better compete in the race of life.

> *"Healing may not be so much about getting better, as about letting go of everything that isn't you—all of the expectations, all of the beliefs—and becoming who you are."*
> *Rachel Naomi Remen*

Answered Prayer

Affirmation: *I believe in answered prayer.*

What does Faith look like to you? My husband, Sandy, says it's "trust on steroids." It has also been said the opposite of faith is not doubt but certainty. I am not certain. I have listened to others talk about their faith and their relationship with God or for Christians like myself, with Jesus. I have heard the stories of the "born again." Many times I am filled with envy and always I am filled with quite a few questions. My faith journey has been slow and persevering, climbing up, slipping down, ever hopeful that I don't slip below my last starting place. I have not found it easy to be faith filled. I have to work at it every day. I appreciate being told, "It's the work of a lifetime." I only hope that my lifetime is long enough to get me to a place where I can fully trust in God's love and care for me and for my loved ones.

I love to read and hear the sermons about God's bountiful love and care for us, His or Her children. There are many preachers who see God as this entity that only wants what's best for us. They lead me to believe that His/Her best is also my best. There is where the difficulty lies. I keep wondering where martyrs fit into this picture of divine love and care.

On February 22, 2011, a group of four Americans were captured and killed off the coast of Somalia. They had been sailing around the world since December 2004 on The Quest, a yacht owned by Jean and Scott Adams from California. The two other Americans on board were Phyllis Macay and Bob Riggle of Seattle, Washington. When I first heard about Jean and Scott, they had been captured by pirates and were being held hostage. They were then surrounded by the US Navy and other helping vessels, but before they could be rescued they were killed. I was truly inspired by their adventurous spirit when I first heard the story of their mission. I know there must be many people who have the same spirit and I just haven't heard about all of them. Jean and Scott were in their 70s and they were sailing to remote parts of the world to share the word of God. I know a lot of people are missionaries and I am usually in awe of anyone who lives a life so far out of most people's comfort zone. They were not what I consider young and here they were so far from their support systems. What would they have done if they got sick, or injured, or needed a dentist? Obviously their mindset was very different from most people but if they died doing God's work, as have so many martyrs, why should I believe that Jesus will take care of me? Oh yes, I would like to believe that. We don't get everything we ask for and sometimes it seems like someone isn't even out there listening. Thankfully sometimes we get something even better than we could have imagined.

I can recall several specific times in my life when I was praying in general for one thing and something so much better came along. It can take my breath away. When my oldest daughter, Melissa, was a single parent we (her father and I) prayed daily for her well-being. We didn't know exactly what that would look like but we knew we didn't want her and her children to endure undue hardship. We were there for them in every way we could be, but we wanted her to be able to care for herself and her children. We wanted her to be independent and self-sufficient in every way possible. Our prayers were answered beyond our wildest expectations when she met Larry Gross. Not only did she find someone amazing with whom to share her life but along with him came two wonderful new grandsons, Joe and Sam.

One day I was overcome with worry about my Mom. I was at a loss about how to help her and she was not capable of helping herself. I was so overwhelmed with the responsibility that I simply turned it over to God. I prayed, "Lord, I do not know what to do. Please send help." Then, I waited. It wasn't long before the phone rang and right after that my family arrived, called and accompanied me to my mom's home. A new on-call physician arrived, and before I knew it, mom was feeling better. I hadn't even had time to stop and thank God for His/Her response. As I reflected later, I began to see the blessings that had been sent and then I had to choose. Was it just the universe stepping into support us? Would it have happened even if I didn't say a prayer? Maybe, but I did pray and it gave me great comfort to believe the help we received was answered prayer. I want to believe in answered prayer. I know I will never understand it, but I believe with every fiber of my being that prayer makes a difference. If I can tap into the belief that my prayers are always answered in a way that only benefits me, think of the peace that can be mine. It has been promised, : "Ask and it will be given to you; seek and you will find; knock and the door will be opened to you" (Matthew 7:7).

I believe God never leaves me if I ask Him/Her to be with me. I'm the one who comes and goes. I believe that through my faith, I will be able to deal with whatever life throws at me and whatever that is, through faith, it will be miraculously transformed into something good, maybe something great, something beyond my wildest imagination. I need to believe. I have chosen to believe. I have chosen the theology and doctrine that I grew up with. It's not perfect, but it enables me to live life with less fear and anxiety than I could without it. I believe it because I want to believe. That's what most of my affirmations revolve around, what I want to believe. In this case I want to believe in a loving caring God. I know the question of how to reconcile a loving God with horrible events has been asked and examined many times around topics even more horrendous than what Jean and Scott endured, like war, famine, child abuse, cancer, and other life-threatening or debilitating diseases. Perhaps, it's not what happens to us, no matter how difficult; perhaps it's how we perceive what happens to us? Perhaps if we practice trusting God, we can go to our death with dignity and grace regardless of the circumstances, knowing that this life is temporary and because of our faith, because of my faith in Jesus Christ I will share in the glory of heaven. My faith and trust in Him will secure me life everlasting with Him and all the Saints and Angels. That's why I believe and why I am still working on it.

Learning to Love Your Life

Affirmation: *I savor life. I glory in life. I love my life!*

I love my life. I haven't always felt that way but I wanted to feel that way and isn't that what affirmations are for, to empower us to create our own reality?

I can remember very clearly the first time I heard someone say, "I love my job." I was a teacher in a rural middle school. I'd been teaching for several years. The gentleman who spoke those words was the English chair of this very small school with only three people in his department. How much money could he have been making? I knew that wasn't the reason for his happiness. I didn't ask him why but over the years I listened for others to say the same thing and yet I very rarely heard it. How often have you heard such a declaration?

Then, one day many years later, I heard a woman say to me, "I love my life." She had shared with me in the past how unhappy she was, so this time I asked why. She had made some very conscious choices and some very drastic changes. She had moved to Italy, took up painting and dancing and fell in love with life. Was it necessary to make such drastic changes in order to love life? Were there other tools she could have used to find happiness without moving to another continent?

My dear friend, Oie Osterkamp, is the director of the Ronald McDonald House in Durham, North Carolina. Most of his life has been dedicated to helping other people. His writing is all about making the lives of others better, richer.

Prior to running the Ronald McDonald House, Oie wrote, *Sharefish* (the opposite of selfish), and founded Sharefish.org, an organization dedicated to bringing hope to the hopeless in Honduras. I don't know the exact number of people who interviewed for the directorship of the Ronald McDonald House but I remember it was a very large number.

My husband and I were with him right after he received the news of his appointment. Of course, he was ecstatic. He told us, "I was born to do this." What a gift to be employed doing something you love.

At the time of this writing, Earline Middleton, is vice president of agency services and programs for the North Carolina Food Bank and has worked there for many years. I came to know her through the Young Women's Christian Association (she and I sat on the advisory board together many years ago). My mom, Margaret Grolimund, was also one of the Food Bank's dedicated volunteers. One day Earline shared that when she first took the job at the Food Bank she had no idea she'd be with them for so long. She said she was "lucky" she had taken a job and found a passion.

We've read about them, we've met them, perhaps we are them: those people who knew from an early age what they were destined for, what they were created to do. Patricia Sprinkle, prolific writer and teacher, shared with our class at the John C. Campbell Folk School that she picked up a career brochure one day when she was fourteen that defined "writer." She finished reading it and thought, "Oh, that's me. I'm a writer," and so she is. Her passion for writing is palpable. It truly is a gift, don't you think, when someone is born with a talent that presents itself to them at any point in their lives, but especially at an early age?

I have always been fascinated by Dale Chihuly, the famous glass sculptor. His works are stunning and massive and he has exhibits all over the world. He once created *The Tower of David* exhibit in a section of Jerusalem. It was one of the most remarkable things I've ever seen, although I had to imagine the full effect by comparing it to another of his exhibits that I actually viewed at the Atlanta Botanical Gardens. I can't imagine how he discovered that he was to be one of the best of such an unusual talent. I think if most people had been born with such a rare gift it would go unfulfilled.

Have you ever heard an adult say, "I don't know what I want to be when I grow up?" It seems to me that's most of the population. But it's never too late. When I facilitate *The Artist's Way* workshops, we use Julia Cameron's process to discover what it is that brings us fulfillment and joy. What nurtured our creative spirit when we were children? What nurtures it now? What is it that we get lost in doing? I have watched many people come through the program with a sense of awe when they discover what they have set aside and almost lost in the name of surviving only to see their passion for their gifts is still there. It's just been lying dormant waiting for a little sunshine to bring it forward.

Sure if I moved to Italy or even went to visit for an extended period, maybe I would feel like my friend. But, perhaps I can create—here and now—a life that I can claim to love. I am the author of my own life. I am the sculptress of how I want my life to look. With some soul searching, prayer, and a supportive community I can shape a life I love. One of the most powerful tools we have is to create a positive affirmation affirming how we feel about our life. Is it possible to change one's feelings about life by simply stating "I love my life"? I decided to try. So, I created the affirmation: ***I savor life. I glory in life. I love my life!*** I claimed it, I wrote it, I read it every morning. Then, it happened. I realized I did love my life. I have surrounded myself with love, love of God, family, friends. My life is amazing and I feel wonderful about it. This is what I believed happened: By the power of my affirmation I slowly began to change. I became more conscious about my decisions, about what I chose to do and not to do, about who I chose to be with and who I did not want in my life. The affirmation worked just like affirmations do. It slowly permeated every fiber of my life and without struggle I was off "living in Italy," painting, dancing, and loving my life.

Financial Prosperity

Affirmation: *We attract financial prosperity.*

I'm fairly thrifty on most things but I don't like to feel like I have to be thrifty. I like to choose to be thrifty. Can you hear the difference? It reminds me of some diets I've been on. As soon as I felt I was denying myself of some specific food, I wanted it more. I once belonged to Weight Watchers Online and I was fascinated by the amount of food I could eat and also that I could eat anything I wanted, within a reasonable amount. It worked fairly well for me. It's the same with money: I don't mind watching my pennies; I just want to do it because I have a responsibility to be financially aware and prudent not because my family is in dire straits. And maybe, just maybe, an ounce of prevention will help keep us from being in real financial difficulties.

The affirmation *"We attract financial prosperity"* is one of the few affirmations in which I include my husband, Sandy. Our finances are totally interwoven. I guess that's fairly normal after more than 40 years of marriage. I remember the first time I told him about this affirmation. I told him it was: *"I attract financial prosperity."* We were in church. He was pretty skeptical. Then the donation basket was passed and I asked him for some additional cash to put in it. Being the great guy he is, he immediately handed me more money. "See," I said, "I do attract financial prosperity!" He smiled and just shook his head.

The topic of money can be a very touchy one. Think about it: almost any topic seems to be fodder for the media. We all seem to know more about people, especially celebrities, than we ever wanted to know but seldom is money, especially someone's income, an open topic. Do you know how much money any of your friends or relatives make? Probably not. It's one of the final taboo subjects of conversation. It's also the number one reason for people to divorce. Many couples come into a relationship with completely opposite ideas about finances. One wants to "save for a rainy day" and another wants to "enjoy the moment." Finding a happy medium appears to be a real stumbling block for many marriages.

My study group, The Seekers, read the book *Second Blooming for Women*.[9] One of the topics led to a lot of discussion both within and outside the group. The statement was, "If money were no object _____." How would you fill that in? I love asking people that question.

My husband has a story about being in speech class in college. He decided to speak about the song "If I Ruled the World."[10] To gather information he went around asking people what they would do if they ruled the world. One person he asked was a young co-worker, the delivery man at their local pharmacy. This young man gave the question a great deal of thought and finally shared, "I would have someone set me up in business." My husband said, "I don't think you get it, "You rule the whole world." The young man again gave it quite a bit of thought and what do you think he answered? "Yup, if I ruled the world, I'd have someone set me up in business. That's what I'd do."

When I was first confronted with the fill-in-the-blank about money, I must admit my vision was limited—not as much as the delivery guy's, but more than I like to admit. Then, after speaking with my group I found myself imagining all sorts of altruistic activities. "no object" you say? "Well, I'd cure cancer, make sure everyone had any proven, available inoculations, feed the hungry—especially the children—and finally, I would make a supreme effort to educate the women of the world." I might have to own a private jet in order to get around tending to the whole world but I'm willing to do whatever is necessary.

Then came the real revelation. Money may be limited but that doesn't mean I couldn't still devote some of my income to those things I feel are important. My donations may not take care of the whole world

---

[9] Kathleen Vestal Logan and E.L. (Betsy) Smith, Ph.D. 2010.
[10] Leslie Bricusse and Cyril Ornadel. 1963.

but they would at least take care of a part of it. I already set aside part of our income to give to charity. As we shared some of our ideas, it came to me that I had also been giving money to educate women. I make a monthly donation to my high school, Saint Agnes Academic High in College Point, New York. It's an all-girl school and I credit it and the teachers I had for the life I now live. It was a wonderful environment. It showed me my potential. I had nuns and lay teachers who had their Ph.D.s in Mathematics, English, and Latin, to name a few subjects. They were remarkable women, and by being in their presence I began to see that I too could educate myself and reach heights I had never dreamed possible.

What about you? If money were no object, what would be your priorities? Remember we are spiritual beings. We have the gifts and ability to tap into the unseen, the unknown … the power of God! Truly, the only limits that exist are the limits we place on ourselves. It's our choice: Do we go to the ocean with a thimble, a bucket, or a pipeline? It's all yours, just like the sun shines on all of us. Prosperity can belong to everyone. Dream large.

FALL

Letting Go of Childhood Limitations

Affirmation: *I let go of my childhood limitations.*

How can one be over the age of 50, 60, or 70 and still be restricted or controlled by emotions and concepts that influenced them as they were growing up? How can one not? I'm speaking about those emotions and concepts that deter us from true joy, that interfere with our ability to completely savor and embrace life. Is it even possible to release oneself, to become an adult in one's own right? Is it possible to grasp the positive qualities that serve us and to acknowledge and appreciate the experience but then let go of those concepts that are damaging us? Part of the creative process encouraged in Julia Cameron's *The Artist's Way* is an examination of what one felt was lacking in his or her childhood. I was a lucky person. Looking back on my childhood, I remember a lot of freedom and amazingly, even with all that freedom I never experienced any trauma. My mother and my father worked very hard. My grandparents lived below our one-bedroom apartment for the first ten years of my life and that was about the extent of our entire family. My father was an only child and my mom's siblings were more than a decade older than she and did not live close to us. I grew up in Jamaica, Queens, New York. When the city was preparing for the 1964 World's Fair, they took down all the trees along my street, Grand Central Parkway, and I could actually see the Empire State Building from my house.

It was not an inner-city neighborhood but it was close. Most of the houses were attached brick homes with the driveway in the back alley.

We had about ten square feet of lawn in the front and my dad paved the entire backyard so we had room to park our cars. My mom had a clothes line that went from the second story kitchen window to a pole out back and she hung most of our laundry out to dry. I would head out to play early in the day and wouldn't return until the street lights came on. We played hard. We skated, rode bikes, climbed walls and trees. We played tag, jumped rope, and played stick ball. In the winter, we ice skated on a pond that was several miles from the house and rode our sleds down the back alley driveways. No one ever seemed to come look for us and if you can imagine, we didn't have cell phones! We were free. We had a lot of choices. I grew up believing I could do anything. I wasn't sure what that was or where it would lead me, but there were no boundaries for me as a child. I assumed there wouldn't be any for me as an adult. Oh, I was well aware of the fact that I was a girl but when it came to running, climbing, and skating, I was equal to any boy. It wasn't until college that I discovered women were expected to only follow certain paths.

In *The Artist's Way*, once you examine what you thought you lacked as a child, you are then encouraged to find ways to parent yourself, to nurture yourself. You can't begin to let go and to heal until you recognize what it is you were missing. Maybe you never felt loved enough. Maybe you never felt valued enough. My parents were so busy that I never felt I received enough affection. Of course, so much of our childhood memories can be so skewed. I once heard the story of a young woman who recalled a fainting episode to her mother. She was shocked to learn she hadn't fainted at all—it had been her sister! Whether or not our feelings are based on reality or perception doesn't matter. They are our feelings. I can still recall childhood incidents that make me feel sad or happy or frightened and my childhood ended more than half a century ago. And now life moves onward. There are times when you need to let go of any junk you feel about your childhood. If you hope to be healthy and happy at some point you simply need to "get over it."

I became my mother's main caregiver in 2012. I was very blessed because at 90 she was still extremely healthy and independent. I'm the oldest of three and mom chose to move near me. She made the move all by herself. She liked to be independent and self-sufficient; it empowered her as it probably does most of us. My prayer for Mom was that she would continue to have joy and maintain dignity as she finished out her life. I only wanted to love her and enjoy her presence. I did, however, still try to be the "good little girl" and make her happy. I wanted to take whatever steps needed to help her feel better. Even in my 60s the child in me still wanted to please my mother, but I knew that no matter what or how much I did I could not please her long-term. I could not make her happy. There is only one person who can make you happy: You.

That's why I create affirmations. It's all up to me what I think, how I perceive life, how I feel. I cannot remain the good little girl and live frustrated and sad because of anyone. I must let go of All my childhood limitations and embrace my own adult determination to create my own happiness. Have you looked at your childhood limitations? Are they interfering with the quality of your life? Can you too release them? Do you want to?

A reporter went to interview a man who was very down on his luck. He had lost everything dear to him and had fallen into a chronic alcoholic state. "Why do you think your life has turned out this way?" he asked. The man shared with him that his father was an alcoholic and he never held out much hope for himself. Then the reporter went to interview the man's brother. He was surprised to find him leading a very happy, successful life. He decided to ask him the same question, "Why do you think your life has turned out this way?" The brother said, "Well, for heaven's sake, my father was a chronic alcoholic. I watched him all through my childhood and decided my life was never going to follow that path."

Life is all about our choices. We get to choose what lessons we want to learn from our childhood. We get to decide if we're going to carry the sad, remorseful feelings with us into adulthood and let them weigh us down or if we are going to learn the lesson, release ourselves from the limitations, and finally grow up healthy and happy. It's never too late.

An Ethical Will

Affirmation: *I discern well between those actions that empower me versus those that enable me and direct my energies towards the former.*

What are you leaving your family when you die? Have you made out a will? Have you written down who will get the silver, the house, and the many treasures you've collected over the years? When we downsized we had an attic and in that attic were many treasures I was sure the "children" would one day want. I had saved their baby furniture. All three children used the same cradle and the same baby carriage. All three children used the same layette set to come home from the hospital. We also had a huge dollhouse that my son and I had built—you know the kind, with a shingled roof and into which people put tiny furniture and lights and decorations. It took us months to glue it all together. We did it on our dining room table. These are just a few of the treasures we had saved over the years. Now, it was time to pass them on to the people we thought would want them. Have you guessed their response? They had no desire to own these items. The baby furniture was outdated and not considered safe any longer. The dollhouse was just too big for their tiny apartments or small homes. The layette may have had a lot of sentimental meaning for me, but they could have cared less about the outfit they wore home from the hospital. Wow! What a learning experience.

All those years of accumulating stuff, caring for stuff, and now getting rid of that stuff. What else did I have, had we been collecting that no one is interested in? There must be something my family, my children, and my grandchildren would like to have. There must be something that I could leave them so they will remember me. Perhaps, the best I could leave them is what life lessons I have learned over these many generations. What are they? What were the most important things

I had learned that I could leave for posterity? What words did I want to use? What sentiments did I want to write down? What would your shared life lessons look like?

The following is my "ethical will"

> Love: Love yourself and love others. It's our first responsibility—our #1 job.
>
> Look for, discover and grow a belief in a Higher Power. Find a way to trust that you can tap into God's love and concern for you as an individual.
>
> Know you are exactly where you are supposed to be at any given moment; practice being in the moment, being in the present.
>
> Write down your priorities; use them to guide you in all your decisions—stay true to them and to yourself.
>
> Write down your dreams. There's power in putting them on paper, energy is born and without struggle they will be manifested. We are always manifesting, beware of your words and thoughts.
>
> Focus on joy.
>
> Focus on compassion and gratitude.
>
> Find a way to see the blessings and benefits in everything that happens to you in life.
>
> Say thank you, thank you, thank you.
>
> Forgive, Forgive, Forgive—yourself and all others.
>
> Smile, Laugh, Play & Dance!!

What does your "ethical will" look like? Give it some thought and write it out. It's small. It takes up very little space. You won't need an attic for it, just a drawer some place and it's a gift that will benefit your family and friends far greater than any piece of old clothing or furniture.

And Then the Wind Chime Rang

Affirmation: *I practice an attitude of gratitude.*

My energy was really low. The house was in the middle of a renovation. We were leaving for a trip that morning and I had received three calls from family members the day before each regarding a different issue and each presenting a fairly serious, if not life-threatening problem. I'd had a terrible night's sleep. It had taken a long time to fall asleep and by 4:00 a.m. I was wide awake. I'd lain there and said the Rosary and all the memorized prayers I knew, and I think I dozed on and off, but by 6:00 a.m. I was wide awake. I silently slipped out of bed because my husband was still resting peacefully, grabbed my daily meditation book and my journal. I put on my slippers and a coverup, made a cup of tea, and headed into the sun room, but it looked like a beautiful warm morning and so I chose instead to sit on the patio.

At the Pink Ribbon Yoga Retreat a few months before this particular day, we were led in a guided meditation by TJ Martin, one of our dedicated founding yoga teachers. Our intention for our yoga-off-the-mat was to help the participants find their heart space, that place where they felt safe and calm. Once they were able to visualize it they were then encouraged to draw it and finally to paint it. Irene Talton, our yoga-off-the-mat facilitator, and TJ showed us how to use the watercolors to achieve our goals, or at least to come close to them for those of us who didn't have a clue how to paint. The guided meditation surprisingly led me to my backyard patio. It wasn't the first time I was stunned by the place a meditation had taken me.

One time many years ago I had been invited by a friend, Dr. James Telfer, to come to his home and to do some "imaging." Once I was in a relaxed state, he too had me imagine a safe place. Whoosh! There I was sitting on a bench in front of the Eseeola Lodge in Linville, North Carolina. My husband and I had visited there many times with very dear friends but I had never considered it a safe or sacred place. I was so surprised to "be" there that I gave a small gasp. I can still remember that session with Dr. Telfer. It was in 1999 but every time I recall it, it's as clear to me now as it was then.

Now I was "on" my patio. We had lived in this particular house for a little over six years. It wasn't my dream house but it's was a good house. It was spacious and I'd had it painted lots of bright colors, yellow being the primary one. We'd spent a lot of time and treasure spiffing it up and making it the way we'd like it to be, but I still missed the house I had left, my former dream home. It was not an attitude of gratitude; I knew it but I was still lacking in thankfulness. Now here I was at the retreat visualizing my sacred space; it could be anywhere in the world or anywhere in my imagination and where was I? On my patio!

As I sat down this morning with my tea and my journal I felt blessed to actually be in my sacred space. It was coolish but I had my hot tea and my coverup so I was comfortable. I opened the journal and began to write. I noted I wasn't well rested and then a stiff breeze blew and the wind chime in the tree rang out. The sound went right into my chest, my heart, and reverberated up and out all of my limbs. I was stunned by the feeling. I stopped writing and listened. There's a small waterfall off to the side of the patio and it was rippling joyfully. The birds were waking up and their chirping was lyrical. Then I heard the young children who live behind me talking with their parents. They were giggling. Tears sprang to my eyes. "Thank you!" I wrote. "Thank you! Thank you! Thank you!"

The day before this epiphany I had walked the local lake with a neighbor friend. I always wondered why she didn't always understand what I said to her. I had decided it was my New York accent and her foreign ears but this morning she shared with me that she had been very ill as a young woman and had lost half of her hearing. It hadn't slowed her down and she went onto a very blessed life, but as I sat there on my patio this morning, I was even more aware of the gift of my hearing. I have continued the practice of listing each morning three joys from the day before. On this morning I listed the joys I had discovered at sunrise: The joy of waking to a new day; the joy of having a sacred space I could actually walk onto; the joy of being married to a man who supports me and my dreams no matter how daunting they may seem; the joy of taking time in the morning to pray and write; and the joy of being the person her family turns to when they need support. I know that's more than three joys. Most mornings there are way more than three. This morning I also listed the joy of the gift of my hearing. My attitude of gratitude had finally overtaken my thanklessness and that sound of the wind chime had pierced not just my chest and my heart but it had pierced and healed my soul.

Outward Bounds

Affirmation: *I embrace stepping outside of my comfort zone.*

I love the television show, *Dancing with the Stars*. I've been a fan since the very beginning. I jokingly say it's because there's no sex, violence, or foul language. I can watch it with my grandchildren or my mother. How many shows are out there that meet those qualifications? I also love to dance.

On the show, about a dozen celebrities learn to dance different ballroom dances with a professional dancer. They wear sparkly, colorful, fun costumes and learn a new dance or two each week until the final week, when one of the couples is declared the champion for that season and they win the famed Mirrorball Trophy. It's such fun to see the people progress. I find it very inspirational. Sometimes there are celebrities who have serious disabilities but they don't let that stop them. In 2011, TJ Martinez won the title. He was a wounded Iraqi war veteran with serious burns to his whole body, including his face. Did that keep him from giving it his all? When I watched him dance and saw the joy that emanated from his whole being, I completely forgot about his disfigurement.

In 2012 Sherri Shepherd, from the television program *The View*, was one of the contestants. She was determined to do well. She wasn't a little lady and I could only imagine how mentally and physically challenging it was for her to learn those dances. She really wanted to win. She was traveling between the show she regularly hosts in New York City and the dancing show in Los Angeles. It must have been a grueling schedule. I know she had all the advantages that money can provide but it didn't lessen the hard work she had to put forth. She was eliminated in week four. She cried and cried but before they could say goodbye she had something she wanted to share with the viewers. "If you don't go towards the thing you fear, you won't be able to say you lived." She went on to say that you should run toward that thing you fear because what you'll find on the other side is simply amazing.

When I mentioned to several of my friends that I was somewhat afraid of my upcoming trip to South America, one of them said, "Oh, Jean, that's great! Because when you come home, you'll feel so good about what you've done." I knew she was right. Her comment gave me a sense of optimism and excitement, instead of dread and anxiety.

My husband and I experienced an Outward Bound course in 2000. We spent five days canoeing through the Everglades. I want to emphasize that I am a city girl: I was raised in Queens, New York; our home was on Grand Central Parkway (I mean, right on it). I was riding the buses and the trains by myself by the time I was ten. The "country" was the property fenced in around the hospitals that bordered our three-block neighborhood. And now, I've been invited by my Brooklyn-born husband to an Outward Bound because he was on the Outward Bound board and thought this was a good idea. I studied about the Everglades; there were snakes and alligators, not to mention other creepy crawly things. But this was the year after I finished treatment for breast cancer and I figured if I could go through that, I could probably canoe through the swamps. I invited a friend to go with us and she was shocked. "What is the purpose of this excursion?" Well, if you needed to ask that, I figured you really didn't need to come along.

So, we went. We brought along our son, Joey, who was in his twenties and our teenaged daughter, Ellen. The good news when we arrived was that we weren't going to be in the swamp; we were canoeing through the Thousand Islands. Whew! On our first night we had to create an island. We took boards from the bottom of the canoes and lashed them together on top of the canoes. This was our "home" for the night and my first night to ever sleep outside under a sky that had more stars than I had ever seen before. I learned a lot during those days. I learned that my daughter was an amazing person. She never complained. She just did whatever was needed. My son was amazing too. My husband was as kind and gracious in the wild as he is in civilization and I learned that I could be an Indian or a Chief. I could both follow and lead, whatever was required. I learned that I could survive in situations I never even imagined. Now when Sandy and I find ourselves doing something that's challenging, outside of our comfort zones, we refer to it as an "Outward Bound experience." It's funny how often we find ourselves in that kind of a position. The purpose of going outside of your comfort zone it to empower yourself. Life is challenging there's no two ways about it. The only way to bolster your confidence is to do those things that frightened you, "to run towards them" as Sherri said. You not only receive the gift of empowerment; many times you find joy and fulfillment from making your way to a whole new place.

Fear is a debilitating disease. I believe we make more decisions based on fear than any other reason. It needs to be recognized and overcome. There's a wonderful tale about a guru who treks all over the land, sharing his wisdom and compassion. One day, he decides to return home. When he walks into his house, he is met by several huge ferocious monsters. They are drooling and their fangs are bared. He looks at them and asks, "Why are you here? What is it that you need?" and half of them disappear. He then asks the others, "Why are you here? Is there something I can do for you?" and they disappear, all except one. He is the biggest and the most frightening of all of them. He is growling and hissing and drooling but the guru is calm. He goes up to the monster and he puts his head into his mouth and with that, the monster evaporates.

This is the challenge: To face our fears with love and compassion, to put our heads into the mouths of life's monsters. Sometimes we get to choose our outward bounds and sometimes they are thrust upon us but if we have faced those events that take us out of ourselves and we've survived, we will be as prepared as possible for those events that we never even imagined.

Passionate for Freedom

Affirmation: *I fully recognize and appreciate the gift of living in a free country and having the privilege of making my choices known.*

> *"Our passions are the winds that propel our vessel. Our reason is the pilot that steers her. Without winds the vessel would not move and without a pilot she would be lost."* Proverbs

Have you ever watched a political convention? As I write this, the 2012 Republican convention has just ended. Politics is not my favorite subject, to say the least. I am a moderate, a middle-of-the-road citizen. I can usually see both sides of an issue and that can leave me very confused about for whom I should vote. I don't have a very successful record. If a friend or family member favors someone for office they would be wise to encourage me to vote for the opponent. I can't ever remember voting for the winner in a major election but I always vote. I may not always be as well-informed as I'd like to be but I always go and cast my vote. I really do try to gather as much information as possible. I read about the different people; sometimes I go to meet them but I've never been so impressed or enamored by a candidate that I was sure I was making the best decision. The best decision for whom: for me, for my country, for the world?

When I vote, I feel like that in itself is the best decision, the decision to exercise my right to vote. When I read about and listen to the sacrifices our ancestors have made and the oppression that still exists in so many countries today, I fully recognize the gift I have been given with the opportunity to choose those I want to represent me, my city, state, and country.

I pray daily for wisdom for our world leaders. There seems to be so many politicians whose only concern is their power and their prestige. Perhaps, that's why I'm not very passionate about politics. I don't have much faith in the people who choose to be politicians. I can't imagine what drives so many of them to put themselves so far out into the public's eye. I wonder, so often, if it's not simply a grand ego trip. I want to believe that a person who is running for office is more concerned about me, his or her constituent, than he or she is about themselves.

When I watch the conventions, the men and women who present themselves with passion about their concerns and about their desires to uplift and empower us, their represented, I am almost relieved. Relieved that someone comes across with what I think is a genuine spirit. It's the people, the audience, with whom I am so fascinated. I am sure there is a selection process for those attendees. I'm sure some have been coming for years, maybe it's a family tradition. I know in many ways it's a fun experience. I've been to several business conventions. The energy generated by a group of people with a common goal is always palpable.

In 2010, my husband Sandy was a keynote speaker for Toastmasters International in Las Vegas. It's an amazing organization and we were very excited to be there. There were over 2000 people there from all over the world. We met people from Africa, Asia, Australia and places that began with many other letters besides "A." It was three days of high energy, lots of stories, and shared visions. I would imagine being at a political convention would be similar. Passion is the word that comes to mind when I watch the people in attendance. Passion! They must truly love and care about the process we have here in the United States to decide our own destiny and they must believe completely in that process. They have devoted time, energy, and talent to participate in the process. I find it inspiring. I believe we all need passion in our lives.

Passion is that quality of life that keeps our hearts beating and our spirits soaring. I believe being passionate about our country, even with its zits, is a worthy pursuit, a just passion. I am proud to be an American. I am grateful to live in a land of peace and freedom. I believe the United States is a place where dreams can come true. I am grateful to be a woman living here in the United States rather than in some oppressive regime. I believe in our compassion as a people and a nation. I value the sacrifices so many Americans have made and continue to make to help others both here and throughout the world.

Vote? For whom will I vote? That's not as important as if I will vote. That choice, no that obligation, is one thing about which I am passionate. There was an article in *USA Today* stating that thousands of Americans didn't plan on voting in the 2012 elections. They simply don't care or they don't believe it will make a difference. Men and women have died, are dying, punished, and being imprisoned because they want— no, they demand—the right to have a voice in their destiny. I will not let this gift, this opportunity, go unused. The United States of America is the greatest country in the world and I for one will exercise my privilege and hope and pray that I cast a vote for someone with passion who will work and lead my country and perhaps our world toward the highest and best we can possibly be.

Giving up the Struggle

Affirmation: *I fully rest in God's care for me. I trust in God's love and I release myself from any struggle.*

Several years ago I met Dr. Ilene Cummings. She was in my life for a very short period of time but had an enormous influence. I first met her when she did several presentations at the local senior center entitled "The Beauty Conversation." The blurb in the catalog indicated this talk had very little to do with physical beauty. She was to do three sessions at a cost of $5.00 a session. I was intrigued. The room was full. Obviously, I was not the only one interested in her topic. There she stood, a woman I guessed to be in her late 80s with long flowing blonde hair and a long skirt worn with boots and bright red nail polish. I was instantly fascinated. This was obviously someone of interest. What would she tell us, and more importantly, what would I learn? I went to all three of her presentations and invited a few friends and my then 80+-year-old mother to join me. It was fun and interesting to be with other women who were looking for ways to find beauty in their lives as aging made society's standard of beauty more and more elusive.

Yes, she stressed the importance of discovering our inner beauty. "Everything accumulates and beauty is the successful result of many years given to the practiced devotion of the classic principles: self-responsibility, courage, integrity, forgiveness, and love." She encouraged us not to let fear limit our dreams and therefore our lives. We shared our stories and we shared what tools we used to create an inner glow so that the appearance of the outer shell took on less importance. It was both fun and informative.

After the sessions were over she offered a more personal session. Once again I was intrigued and so a dear friend of mine and I invited Dr. Cummings for coffee and whatever she had in mind. She showed up in what was by now her usual flamboyant style, driving a red convertible sports car and carrying several lovely prints of ethereal looking women. After a short time, she invited each of us to look at the prints and to see ourselves in them. We chose three of them, one each to represent the past, present, and future. After some meditative guidance, we imagined we were the angelic-looking beings in the prints and we were invited to speak to the woman in the print that represented the past.

At one time there was a television advertisement for an investment company where people encountered their future selves and shared their past knowledge and experience with themselves. In one of the ads a man met himself on a plane. He sits down and shares the successful investment strategy he has used and then the older self gets up and moves to another seat. "Where are you going?" the younger self asked. "To first class." The older self replied, "Because of my wise investments I can afford it." We learn so many lessons as we go through life. Everything seems clearer in hindsight.

Dr. Cummings asked me to speak aloud what lesson I wanted to impart to my younger self. Of all the things I'd done and learned what was the most important thing I wished I'd known ahead of time? What information, other than the mega jackpot lottery numbers or the success of some very successful stock buy, did I want to impart to my youthful self that would perhaps make my life richer and more rewarding?

I am a hard worker. I am steady and persevering. Give me a project and I will complete it. I believe it was these qualities instilled by my parents that enabled me to complete my education. I find myself looking around and seeing what might make my world a better place and then I step out and take on those projects. I strive and I think that has led me to this amazing life I now have the privilege of living, but I also struggle. I struggle because I forget that it's not all up to me. I do not have to be in complete control of everything I decide to do. In reality, I am never in complete control of everything on which I'm working. I know I have to do my part, like the farmer who tills and plants the fallow ground but without God's help there will never be any reaping.

The lesson I chose to share with my younger self was to work hard but to let go of all the struggle. I wanted her to know she should embrace and enjoy every moment of her life. Let go of the worry, the anxiety, the fear. She needed to stop trying to control everything and rest and relax more. I wanted her to know, without a doubt that if she learned to trust her inner divinity, the Spirit of God, she would strive less and attain more.

Therefore, my affirmation, my intention became: ***I fully rest in God's care for me. I trust in God's love and I release myself from any struggle.*** I call it the "RTR principle:" Rest-Trust-Relax.

There is, however, as Suzanne Rives, one of my wise friends, pointed out to me, one more part to this: I must also be open to receive. I like to help. I like to give. For me, it is humbling to be on the other side of generosity. One of the great lessons I learned from breast cancer was how to be humble and to receive graciously the care of others. Humility is a hard lesson. My friend reminded me of God's generosity. Her suggestion reminded me of all that is available in the divine realm and how important it is for me to stay open to God's love and bounty. So I guess the principle needs to be retitled the "RTR-Receive" Principle.

What advice do you have for your younger self? It's not too late. We are younger now at this moment than we will ever be again. Seize the opportunity, take the time to have a dialogue, and go forward wiser and more adventurous. Go forward living a more beautiful life.

Love and Grief

Affirmation: *I am a spiritual being having a human experience.*

What do you think happens after someone dies? It's interesting that we here in America seem to act like death isn't a reality. I often get the impression that most Americans simply avoid the topic. I wonder if most people believe that as long as they don't think about it or talk about it, it won't happen.

My dad, Frank Grolimund, died when I was 34. He was 62. He died from a glioblastoma brain tumor. At the time, I didn't recognize how young we both were. Now that my age has passed his by several years I am fully aware of how young he was. The diagnosis was a mystery to us and to him. The doctors performed surgery and then we had one meeting with his doctor who explained to us that my dad would be all right for a short while and then the tumor would return. He didn't explain what that meant but we knew it wasn't a good thing. He never told us, "He's going to die." I'm not sure we would have heard him or believed him. My dad was not in the room for this conference and no one came to offer us guidance about how to deal with all this. He died about 18 months after the surgery. His death had a profound effect on my life. I don't think I ever stopped thinking about death after he died. He had such a zest for life, it was remarkable! He was my hero and I loved him dearly. It's been over 30 years and it still makes my heart ache that he's no longer on this earth.

My father-in-law, Joe Costa, also died of a glioblastoma brain tumor. It was 20 years later but not much had changed, except now we knew what it was and we knew what the doctor meant when he told us after the surgery that it would return. I, for one, had no doubt about what the doctor was telling us. My father-in-law fought a valiant battle with his wife, Yolanda, next to him every step of the way. He also died about 18 months after receiving the initial diagnosis. He, too, was a remarkable man very much loved by his family and many friends.

I have many other friends and relatives who have died but these two men were dearest to me. My father's death left me with a sense of urgency. I fully recognized that I didn't want to miss a thing. I also don't put many dreams on hold. One of the questions in my monthly review is, "What did you want to do that you didn't get to do?" I must admit most months I don't have an answer to the question. Most months if I had something I wanted to do, I went and did it. I know there may not be a next month. That was the gift I was left with after my father's death. I was left with an awareness of how important life is today. I've been gifted with the appreciation of the people I love and how fragile their existences are.

Sometimes there are concentrated periods of time when death is more present than others. There was one two-week period in my life when I received notice of two friends dying, the mother of another friend and the sister-in-law of another. During that time, I was also invited to sing for our church's Resurrection Choir. The funeral was for a 75-year-old woman. I kept it together until the dead woman's daughter hugged her father and the deceased's husband of 57 years. 57 years! That's a lifetime! How does one go on? How do widows and widowers do it? How do parents who lose a child continue to live?

As an MSW (Masters in Social Work) intern at Hospice of Wake County, I was one of the bereavement counselors. I had been a patient care volunteer for years and was very excited to be accepted into their organization. What I observed during my time with Hospice and have continued to see is that people heal from grief. Some people heal more quickly than others but at some point people get back to living their lives. It's actually one of the five stages of grief, first introduced by Elisabeth Kübler-Ross in her book *On Death and Dying*. It's the last stage, "acceptance."

In the Irish movie *A Shine of Rainbows* a widower is left with the care of a young boy that his wife wanted to adopt. The young woman who died loved color. She had red hair and bright green eyes and she wore bright rainbow-colored clothing and decorated her home with lots of bright colors. One day the young boy comes home from school to a house denuded of all the woman's things. The husband has gathered them all together and is burning them. The young boy runs to the fire and saves his "mom's" favorite scarf. They grieved in two very different ways. One was trying to erase all his memories (which, of course, one cannot do) and the other was trying to hold onto all of them (which, of course, one cannot do). Eventually, they find healing. They found it by sharing the love they both have for their dead loved one. They come full circle and you can see them entering the final stage of grief; healing is taking place.

That was the wonderful part of being a bereavement counselor, I could see people heal. It left me with such a sense of hope. There are so many strong, brave, loving people who have suffered such loss and grief but who manage to continue to live full, rich lives. It's inspirational.

For me, the greatest gift my faith has given me is a belief in the afterlife or perhaps a better phrase is the eternal-life. I believe we are pure spirit and while our bodies die our spirits live on. In *The Power of Positive Thinking*, Norman Vincent Peale writes, "Another profoundly curative element in the prescription for heartache is to gain a sound and satisfying philosophy of life and death and deathlessness. When I gained the unshakable belief that there is no death, that all life is indivisible, that the here and the hereafter are one, that time and eternity are inseparable, that this is one unobstructed universe, then I found the most satisfying and convincing philosophy of my entire life." I too believe as he does. While the heartache of losing a loved one can be unbearable, the belief that they are not gone, but in a place I cannot yet be, brings me comfort and with that comfort, acceptance.

Worry and Anxiety

Affirmation: *I avoid all thoughts that weaken me.*

Do you ever feel anxious? Do you ever wake up in the middle of the night with so many things on your mind you can't get back to sleep? If you don't you must already have developed a system that keeps you calm and centered. It's not something you can develop when you're in the throes of what is or appears to be a crisis. It must be something, some tool you've created and used regularly when you felt calm. Then when you are not feeling calm, you use that tool and your body responds with the conditioned reflex, relaxation.

I had a friend tell me that he had a *mantra* (a repeated phrase or word) he used every time he was at the airport (one of his most stressful environments) but it really didn't seem to make any difference. He didn't see what purpose it served. He never felt any calmer. I asked him if he used this tool at any other time and he said, "No." Can you see the problem with this? Every time he found himself stressed he repeated the same phrase. He conditioned his response to anxiety. He needed to practice his mantra when he was feeling calm and centered.

People I know use meditation to create this sense of peace, others use prayer. Many in the catholic faith say the Rosary, a set of Our Fathers and Hail Marys that are repeated over and over while moving one's fingers along a set of beads. Many meditators finger beads, called *mala* beads, while they repeat their mantras.

When I was going through radiation, it was an extremely stressful situation and I was very anxious. I also didn't feel too well so that added to the anxiety. One of the Duke Cancer Patient Support counselors set up an appointment with a nurse practitioner named John Seskavitch. In my experience, John was a unique nurse. He focused on healing the whole person, mind, body, and spirit. He had already created several meditation tapes and sponsored many mind-body workshops. He sat with me and asked me about my faith, my practices and then suggested I repeat the Hail Mary during treatment.

My walks take me around Apex Lake, a beautiful path close to my home here in North Carolina. I've walked it for over twenty years and often use the quiet time to say the Rosary. I dedicate each decade (a group of ten Hail Marys and one Our Father) to a specific group of people: My family and friends, my church group, the support people in my life, all those special intentions I have in my heart, our military and their loved ones and our world leaders (I figure they could use all the help they can get with the condition of the world today). As soon as I laid down for my radiation treatment after that first session with John and began reciting the Hail Mary, I was no longer anxious. I was "on the path" around Apex Lake! The sun shimmered on the water, the geese and ducks called out, the great blue herons stood perfectly still in the water, people nodded and said, "Good Morning!" and I was calm and all was well.

I once read about someone who kept a "worry box." All week long, if something came up that he was concerned about, he would put it in the box and he'd tell himself that he'd worry about it on Friday at 5:00 p.m. Each Friday he'd go to the box and lay out all his concerns. What do you think happened? Most of his concerns had been addressed, had been resolved. Part of my journaling practice is to look back each month and do a general review of how my life went. One of the questions I ask myself is, "What was something I worried about that I don't worry about now?" There's always an answer that reflects something that's been resolved or even more profound, something that never even came into reality.

George Burns, the famous comedian, once said he never worried; it was a useless waste of his time. "Why would I worry about something I can do something about? I'll just go do it. And, why would I worry about something I have no control over?"

Not worrying takes practice. If you've developed the worry habit, you can develop the habit to not worry. You can find some tool, some process that will effectively help you control your anxiety. One of those tools is affirmations, like ***"I avoid all thoughts that weaken me."*** Turn your thinking around. Use your quiet time to assure yourself that all is well, all is well! Take God's peace and love and your sense of well-being with you out into your life and into the world. It's the work of a lifetime but it's well worth it, don't you think?

Put Your Glasses On, Change Your Vision

Affirmation: *I am a lifelong learner.*

Our vision is a gift and one of my most valued senses. How we see the world colors our whole attitude. Have you ever heard "It's 10 percent aptitude and 90 percent attitude"? What about the difference between an optimist and a pessimist? "A pessimist is right 100 percent of the time." We get to choose, moment to moment, whether or not we will see the glass half full or half empty. What if we could simply put on a different set of spectacles to help us change our perspective?

There are people who want to expand their view of the world and then there are those who want to stay in their safe places. Unfortunately, it's easier to stay "safe," especially as one ages. If you're not careful your world can become smaller and smaller. You may start making choices to stay safe which begin to limit your experiences. One must make a conscious choice to continue to learn and to grow. I once heard it said, "You can be green and growing, or ripe and rotten. " It's your decision.

It's helpful to be able to see when we want to move forward. Sometimes, however, it's more important to look back, to see where you've been and what you've learned from the road previously taken. No matter in what direction we are looking or from what vantage point, high or low, we can use our vision to enhance our experiences. At one of the International Toastmaster's convention one of the speakers used the topic "The Click that Sticks" to talk about his life experiences and how instead of trying to capture everything on a camera lens, he chose to imagine his eyes being the camera and recording the event onto his brain, making it "the click that sticks."

I wonder if people's height has anything to do with how they see the world? I know I love being up high. I love it when I have the opportunity to look at the world from a plane, a mountain, or even a hill. I'm only five feet tall, so usually my vantage point is upward. One day many years ago at a NCAA basketball tournament I left my seat during intermission to find a pay phone (OK so this was many, many years ago) and call home. The sign for the phone was several yards up ahead at the end of this very long line. My view was so limited that I could barely see the top of the sign because of all the tall men in front of it. I was surprised so many people needed to use the phone, until I got closer. I was in line for the men's room. My vision had been so limited, I wasted time waiting on the very wrong line.

At some point in our lives most of us find ourselves wearing glasses to help us see. Some need glasses at an early age, others not until they are older. There are many different types of eye conditions that require some help to allow people to see clearly. Sadly, for some, glasses can't help at all; they are blind.

Have you ever been in complete darkness, no little LED lights anywhere, no moonlight, nothing but blackness? I once participated in a smoke lodge ritual. The rocks were heated for several hours before they were placed in the center of a makeshift tent. Once the inside of the lodge reached a sauna-like temperature we were invited into the session. The heat enveloped us and began to immediately soothe any aching muscles. Then, they closed the flap. I couldn't breathe! Suddenly, the heat felt like I was being wrapped in a heavy flannel blanket, from head to toe. "Deep breath! Deep breath!" I told myself. Then I noticed there was a tiny bit of light seeping in under the edge of the flap. I was saved! I found my breath.

Helen Keller was blind from birth. She was not only blind, but also deaf. Her story, so well known from the film *The Miracle Worker*, tells the tale of a young girl completely isolated from society because of her disabilities but with the help of a gifted and dedicated teacher, Anne Sullivan (who was also blind) she became a world-renowned author, political activist, and lecturer. She was the first deaf-blind person (man or woman) to earn a Bachelor of Arts degree. She had "vision" even though she did not have sight.

One of my efforts to stay green involved going to a writing workshop hosted at the John C. Campbell Folk School. The instructor, Patricia Sprinkle, asked us to write a description of a familiar place. Seven students sat in the cozy "writing lab" overlooking the green meadows and tree-covered mountains. It was the beginning of fall and the trees had just begun their colorful metamorphosis. We all wrote about some place we knew well and then we shared our stories but we had left things out, things like the doors and the windows of our familiar places, things that we saw all the time but had stopped noticing. The instructor suggested we put on our "writer's glasses" to enable us to see things in a new light.

In one of my church study groups we worked on how to improve our relationship with God. One of the women told a story about wearing her "blessings from God" glasses. She said she imagined them to be rose tinted and enabled her to more easily see the gifts God bestowed on her on a daily basis. Later, when our writing instructor at the JCCFS told me to put on "my writing glasses" that enabled me to see the world differently than I was used to seeing it and helped me see it from more than one vantage point and/or renewed that view which had become familiar to me.

I like the idea of putting on different lenses to see different things in my life not only more clearly, but differently. Perhaps that's what it was like for Helen Keller. Even though she couldn't see and she couldn't hear, she put on the "glasses" that Anne Sullivan created for her and she was able to see the world in so many different ways, perhaps more clearly than many of us sighted people.

Shakespeare wrote, "The eyes are the windows to the soul." What happens to our soul when we put on different glasses? Anything? Does it expand and grow? Does it change color, become kinder, warmer? Does our expanded vision bring us closer to our spiritual self, to our God? The answer is: It's up to you. You get to choose what you want to see and how you expect it to impact your life. My newest pair of glasses to don were my "writer's glasses" and I was very curious to see what my new "glasses," my new vision, would reveal to me. What about you? Is there anything you're interested in seeing from a different perspective? It doesn't have to be a new subject for which you might need different glasses; perhaps it's a relationship or it might be a philosophical perspective. Put on your new glasses, change your vision, broaden your horizons. It may just be the tool you, too, need to see your dreams or concerns in a whole new way.

Easy to Unhook

Affirmation: *I embrace the concept of being "easy to unhook."*

In Ecuador, in the home of my daughter-in-law (my *nuera*) there is not a television in the living area. In fact, when I visited her relatives' homes in Ecuador none of them had a television in the main living area. I know that there are homes in many parts of the world that cannot afford a television so that's the least of their issues, and I know there are some homes in the United States who also keep their living areas television free. A couple of my friends actually have this practice but when I visited Ecuador I had the privilege of staying with my daughter-in-law's mother (my *consuegra*, the Ecuadorian word that describes my relationship with her), sometimes for extended periods. (The simple fact that they have a word for the mother or father of their son or daughter's in-law is an example of how different their culture is than ours.)

Our home, my husband's and mine, is not television free. We have managed to keep the television out of the bedroom, but it has a strong presence in our kitchen. When the families in Ecuador gather, their main activity is conversation. I was lucky enough to be invited to the home of one of the aunts to enjoy *fanesca*, a traditional potato soup. We were away from the city and her family was gathering for this traditional Ecuadorean feast, celebrated after Easter week (*Semana Santa*). In the past all the farmers would come together after they harvested their grains, different farmers grew different types of grains and each family would contribute their harvest to the fanesca (the soup also traditionally contains many different types of beans). The celebration I attended had a fruit salad as its first course.[11] After the fruit came the soup. When

---

[11] In Ecuador the variety of fruit is amazing; I was told there are 40 different types of bananas.

the fanesca was served I was amazed that they had enough dishes and glasses to serve everyone, no paper or plastic. The accoutrements for the soup included empanadas, pickled vegetables, hard-boiled eggs, and some sort of fish that looked like flaked tuna but tasted much saltier. You decided if you wanted all or some of the sides to put into your soup. I tried them all but I had been forewarned about eating too much of the grain-bean entree because visitors didn't necessarily digest the soup easily. After the soup came birthday cake and ice cream (I knew I could digest that just fine).

At the aunt's home there were three buildings. The first was the home of her son and his family. Then there was her home. It was a simple stone building with one bedroom. There is no heat or air conditioning. If it's cold, you close the windows; if it's hot, you open them. The third building was the family gathering space. The day I visited there were around 30 people of all ages. When we arrived, I (a complete stranger) was kissed by everyone there who could walk. If someone was chatting with another or sitting down or running around playing, their activity came to a halt and they came over to greet us.

We were there about four hours. We talked and then we talked some more. Most of the adults made an effort to come over and sit with me and let me share some of my visit in my halting, stumbling Spanish. The really good news was that many of them were fluent in English. I also watched. The children, even the teenagers, either ran around playing outside or just gathered and talked. There weren't any electronic gadgets being used by anyone. Although many of the adults had cell phones, few of them paid any attention to them. I wondered if the existence of the cell phone was the beginning of the demise of this delightful "unhooked" tradition.

Everywhere we went during my visit it was the same. Warm greetings from all and people who seemed to value time and connecting to each other more than what was going on somewhere else or what was coming next. Most evenings at home with my host family, we sat and talked, or my daughter-in-law spent hours helping me with my Spanish. One evening four of us, including the teenaged granddaughter, sat and played cards. It was delightful.

I had been thinking of redoing my living room to include one of those big-screen televisions that they show in all the commercials. We have a television but it's behind a cabinet and it's seldom used. After my Ecuadorian experience, I began wondering if I shouldn't remove it and the kitchen television and try life "unhooked." I wonder if our family gatherings would include more talking or if everyone would simply go off to find their personal way of connecting somewhere else. My eldest daughter and her husband and his boys are good at being present with family and friends. I wonder if it's a personality trait, a cultural trait, or if it's something that can be learned? I wonder if our American culture will allow us to "unhook"? I find myself worrying about us losing the art of visiting and communicating.

The cartoon film *Wall-E* was a satire about what will happen to us in the future if we don't make an effort to change. In the film the people of Earth were living on a space ship because they had wrecked the planet. Their arms and legs no longer functioned because they had floating recliners, and in front of them they had floating monitors for communication. They weren't even aware of the people next to them until a rogue robot, Wall-E appeared and kept upsetting everything.

I know our monitors and chairs are not floating, yet, but have you watched people on the streets or in the airports or at parties? How many times have you been talking with someone when their cell phone rang and they answered it like you weren't even there or they acted like the person calling was more important than you? Once again I am being asked to stay present in the moment and to the people I am with. My daughter-in-law describes my son, an information technologist, as someone who is "easy to unhook." He doesn't even take his phone with him when he plays golf. I think that's great!

Now, there's a goal, to be "unhooked." Actually, I'm pretty good at it. The issue, and that's another story, is that I also want my whole family to be unhooked, but I know I am not in charge of changing anyone except myself. I think if I suggested removing the television from the kitchen some in my family would revolt. I thought maybe I could just cover it with a towel and try doing without for a week or two. I also considered putting a basket by the front door in which people can drop their gadgets. I then wondered if anyone would come visit us anymore? What if I promised to still feed them? What if I promised they could retrieve them at any time as long as they used them outside the house, like most public places do with cigarettes? I could see it already, most of my family standing on the front steps or in the driveway until I finally called "dinner is served!"

Miraculous Happenings

Affirmation: *My life is Joy-filled; Miracles occur, love surrounds me and permeates every aspect of my existence.*

We all know that in *Alice in Wonderland*, Alice jumps down a rabbit hole into an unknown, full-of-adventure, self-examining world. Sometimes we are pushed down that hole and sometimes we choose to jump, but either way we get to decide what we'll learn and what we'll take away from our experiences.

After being treated for breast cancer in 1999, I was left feeling very unsure of what I should be doing for myself. During the intense treatment, which for me lasted almost a year, I was well cared for and in constant contact with my doctors and other caregivers. Then the day came when I was "released." I had my last radiation treatment and threw an End of Radiation Celebration. Sure, I was scheduled for follow-up mammograms and yearly checkups but other than that I was on my own. Yes, in many ways we are always "on our own" as we go through cancer but for me, being released, while a reason for celebration, was also very scary. I began looking for those things that might help me feel supported, educated and uplifted.

As a long-time yoga practitioner, I turned to the yoga world to see what might be out there. It was in 2000 that I made my first trip to Kripalu Yoga Center in The Berkshires of Massachusetts (where I ultimately returned for my yoga teacher training). It was there that I had the thought about creating a yoga retreat for breast cancer survivors. I envisioned several days at the beach, practicing yoga, resting, swimming, talking, and breathing! In 2005, the first Pink Ribbon Yoga Retreat (PinkRibbonYoga.org) for women breast cancer survivors became a reality. My jump down the rabbit hole had taken me to one of the most amazing, fulfilling adventures of my life.

As of 2012, a few hundred women have experienced all the things I envisioned and so much more than I ever imagined. This retreat has been spirit driven and Divinely blessed since its inception. Have you ever been involved in something like this, something that takes on a life of its own, something that comes together and blossoms with a miraculous aura?

I have never approached an individual or an organization that has not generously agreed to help us in whatever way they could. The first person to say yes was Rhonda Bailey, a yoga instructor and friend. She set the standard for everyone else. After that, with the support of the Duke Cancer Patient Support Program, we were ready to go. Our teachers generously volunteer their time and talent. Our friends and family come forward every year to help defray the costs and to provide scholarships for those who are unable to pay. One woman donates cushy beach towels for everyone. We have had homemade biscotti and pound cake. A local ice-cream shop donates sundaes for everyone and one of our committee members makes the supreme effort to go taste several of the flavors beforehand. Every year we raise enough money with the efforts of my husband, Sandy, to help pay for anyone who wants to come on scholarship. It's phenomenal how it all comes together and it's obvious to all of us there that the success of this event is beyond anything most of us have ever experienced. It has to have the hand of God in it.

Who comes to a retreat like this? Obviously women who have experienced breast cancer (although we have many people who want to come but don't want to qualify to come). But really what type of individual attends an event like this? I am here to tell you, they are amazing individuals. They come from all over the country. Most of the women have heard something about what goes on but it really is an unknown entity. Many have never practiced yoga; many come without knowing anyone else. Some are in the middle of treatment; others have been out of treatment for years. They don't know what the accommodations are like, who their roommate may be, or what the food is like, but they come anyway. They are the type of people who aren't afraid to jump down the rabbit hole. They are amazing, brave, adventurous human beings and when we gather we get to share the adventure.

The focus of the retreat, believe it or not, is not breast cancer. Yes, we all have that in common, and yes, the subject comes up and people share experiences, and more often than not, they share what worked for them. The focus of the retreat is living life to the fullest. Each year, as in most yoga practices, we take an intention. The first year the intention was that it be "a joyful experience for everyone involved." One year we focused on an "Open Heart." We also took the intention to "Stay in the Moment." In 2008, our intention was to "Marvel in the Mystery."

The retreat provides multiple healing modalities. Besides yoga, which in itself is multi-dimensional; there's the ocean, art-therapy, massage therapy, silent walks, and Yoga Dance. Some people relate to some and not to other modalities. Other people need a little bit of all of them but either way they all lead to an increased sense of well-being and support.

We begin and end the retreat with a Sharing Circle, everyone comes together and each person is invited, although not required to speak. I'm sure there are many such rituals involved with other gatherings but I was introduced to this ritual at Kripalu. There are many guidelines. The first, of course, is confidentiality. We go on to talk about using the "I" word, not the community "we." Only one person is allowed to speak at a time and it's highly recommended that everyone actively listen and not plan what they might want to say. In between each speaker we take a collective in breath and sigh it out. We imagine clearing the psychic white board in the middle of the circle. There are other suggestions but these are the main ones. What happens during the circles? What happens during the four days? Miracles occur!

Miracles, you say? What is miraculous about ice cream, beach towels, and homemade goodies? Well, for one thing they simply appear like the manna in the desert in the bible story. We never ask for these treasures but what is really miraculous is what happens to the mind, body and spirit of each of the ladies and our one man (the breast cancer counselor for the Duke Cancer Patient Support Program, Geoff Vaughn). By the end of the four days a light comes on in each person. There has been healing; there's been a renewed sense of hope. The women have found camaraderie and acceptance. We have laughed, cried, played, swam, created, danced, and practiced yoga. We have found the power in each of us and as a group. The event is laced with miracles, especially the overwhelming feeling of love that permeates each person including me, as the retreat comes to a close.

Time is My Friend

Affirmation: *Time is My friend.*

Many years ago while I was waiting in a shop for service, there was also an older gentleman waiting. When the time came for the next customer, he motioned for me to go ahead of him. I protested even though I was in a hurry. He insisted. Then he said to me, "Time is my friend." This was my first affirmation and I have been writing it, reading it, and saying it to myself ever since I began practicing positive affirmations. I must say, it is one of my most challenging.

I try to live in "divine time" as my dear friend and healer, Valerie Kelly, called it. Divine time is where I simply go through my day knowing that everything will simply fall into place, not worrying about when I leave or when I arrive or if I'm late or early … but that's a very rare event. Most of the time I am struggling with getting it all in. I want more time! I believe Valerie's healing touch began before I ever arrived for my appointment. My appointment was usually sometime around 2:30 in the afternoon. Many times when I arrived, Valerie wasn't ready to see me. At first I was annoyed. This was just not how things are done in my world. You choose a time and a place and then you arrive at that agreed time or at least close to it. Truly, I have been in knots most of my life trying to be on time. I usually begin getting tense just knowing I have a destination to which I am supposed to arrive at a particular time, long before I've even begun the journey.

Valerie didn't get it. She lived in her own space. She began her massage sessions when she was ready and she never ended them until she felt you were complete, not when the clock reached a certain point. As the years went on, I found myself responding to her sense of time. If I was going to be late, I wasn't the least bit worried. I'd usually text her and tell her when I thought I'd arrive and she'd let me know, without fail, that that was just fine. If I were early she'd sit me in her lovely living room and let me just rest or we'd chat while she finished lunch or settled the dog down. I know she had clients that couldn't adjust to this approach but I so valued her healing skills that I decided to make it work. I was so relaxed when I arrived that my body was completely receptive to her gifts. One of her gifts to me was the gift of my not having to watch the clock and in return my gift to her was accepting her exactly the way she was, a radiant being who wouldn't let the world confine her.

As I get older, I am finding time goes faster and faster. Have you had that experience? As I write this, it is the fall of the year and I can't imagine where the year has gone. I heard a poem once that best expressed this sentiment to me: "I woke up, turned my head and when I looked back, it was 30 years later." After sharing this with a friend, she added, "or 40 or 50!" There's a very old movie called *Stop the World I Want to Get Off*. That's how I feel most days. I want time to stop. I want to savor each and every moment. I want more time, today and forever.

I have another friend who lost both her daughter and her husband to cancer. One day she told me she knew we all had to die; she just didn't expect life to go so quickly. We cried! How do you make peace with that? I know time is a manmade tool. I know there are all kinds of theories about how it doesn't really exist; that it's supposed to be more like a layer cake, one field lying over another. I used to tell people, "Time is not my friend."

I once read that a man from a tribe in a foreign land told an American, "You have so many watches, but no time. We have no watches, but plenty of time." That's how I want to feel like I always have plenty of time. I want to treasure each moment. I don't want to worry and rush about. I don't want to think about tomorrow when I haven't even gotten out of bed today. I hope that by believing time is my friend, life will be easier, richer, and more joyful.

How do you make peace with time? Can part of it be believing this life is not going to end; we will live on in another dimension, maybe one of those layers the physicists write about. In the meditation book, titled meditation book, *God Calling*,[12] the opening reading states that God designed humans to live only one day at a time. I wonder if God didn't design us to live one moment at a time? Ah, there it is again, the call to meditate. The call to stay connected to exactly what is happening right now, not planning for the future or ruminating on the past.

Sharon Salzberg, one of the founders of the Insight Meditation Center in Barry, Massachusetts, told the story at a workshop I attended about an intense training session she once underwent with a meditation master. She was to report to him daily about her meditation practice. She said the first time she showed up with her notes he didn't let her speak before he asked her "Did you brush your teeth today?" "Yes," she replied. "Did you pay attention to the experience?" She had not. The next time she arrived he again spoke before she could begin to share all her insights she'd learned during her meditation sessions. "Did you walk here today?" "Yes," she answered. "Did you pay attention to the experience?"

Perhaps that is part of the secret, paying attention not rushing about, not being pre-occupied with the business, many times the trivia, of life. My dear friend, Valerie, knew this and she gifted me with her concept of life, time, and love. It's a good thing she knew how to stay in the moment and live each day to the fullest because she lost her life at the age of 53. I have many emotions attached to her memory, but one that makes me smile is thinking about my arrival at her home for my appointment; calm, centered, and knowing that whatever time I arrived was the perfect time. What about you? Is time your friend or your enemy? May you too discover the gift of living (at least occasionally) in divine time. May you discover the gift of joyfully living in perfect time.

---

[12] Arthur J. Russell, 1995.

Healthy Mind, Healthy Body

Affirmation: *I invite God's divine healing light into my mind, body, and spirit, creating a state of total well-being.*

One day someone asked me if I liked my body. I said, "No." Afterwards I was so disappointed in myself. I've been affirming for years how much I value my body, but my gut reaction to the question in no way reflected my intention. Not only am I an integral part of American society with all the hang-ups presented to us through the media about the female image, I have also had quite a bit of pain—not to mention, cancer. I haven't always felt safe in my body especially after breast cancer. I mean I was feeling great; I wasn't sick, and then there was a great "boom" and I was diagnosed with cancer, operated on, loaded up with chemicals, and radiated!

During a visit to one of my chiropractors, our discussion turned to healing one's self. She spoke to me about how the beliefs we have concerning our health have a direct impact on our state of well-being or our ill-being. She has a practice she uses to make life changes. She explained that not only did she find a phrase or sentence to affirm the desired change, but she also took time to visualize it. I left with a newly found sense of power. I had been struggling for years with a sense of anxiety about my health—especially with a sore hip—and here I was being told that I could make change just by thinking differently about it. I'd been practicing affirmations for years, but I never thought about re-framing the ache in my hip.

Then, I reread John Sarno's book *Healing Back Pain*. There it was again, the same message. How you think about your body and your health has a direct effect on its state. At one point in the book, Dr. Sarno says that you either believe the theory or you embrace it simply because you're so desperate for relief. I happen to fall into the first category. I know one must be careful believing we are fully responsible for everything that happens to us. It can lead to a "blame the victim" mentality but I choose to think I am responsible for almost everything that happens to me. However, sometimes forces beyond our control overcome our best intentions. Believing that can be scary but it also takes away the blame. I read that people who think of themselves as resilient have fewer health problems (I wonder if they have fewer problems all together).

After talking to my chiropractor and re-evaluating how I visualized my body, I decided it was time to change my thinking and came up with the above affirmation. Oh, but there's much more to it. I also told myself, "I am strong, resilient, flexible, and powerful ..." and many more words that affirmed my body in a positive light. When I took the time to closely examine how I could feel about my body, I realized I was only focusing on the negative and had totally neglected the positive aspects, like the fact that most of my body does not hurt or that I have produced the miracle of three healthy children. My body is a miracle unto itself. I understand so little of how it operates, but it does; most of it is in good working order, miraculously. So, I am making a very conscious effort to value my body, to believe in its ability to heal itself, to be strong and healthy. I believe the process begins by loving my body.

An article in *USA Today* reported on a study to help women increase their sexual desire. Apparently there are many, many women who are interested in this because this study involved several hundred of them. As in most studies, there was a control group. This group was told they were taking a "magic" elixir that would do all they would hope it would do. It was, however, a placebo. Can you guess what happened? Most of these women had a marked increase in their level of desire. This study took place over several months and their levels did not decrease. I don't know if they were ever told it was a placebo and for all I know they are all still out there enjoying themselves without knowing it's all in their minds, but that's just the point. What else is just in our minds? What else can we change to our benefit by simply believing it is true? That's the purpose and secret of positive affirmations; say it as if it already is;

believe it as if it's already true. Fake it until you make it! It's without a doubt a great way to live your life. Want to be sexy? Well, if that's one of your intentions, go for it. If hundreds of women can feel that way by simply taking a sugar pill, certainly it's available to those of us who decide to choose to believe it to be true.

The message is clear. How you think has a direct impact on how you feel. So, the next time someone asks me if I love my body I know I will say, "Yes." I affirm: ***I have an awesome body. I invite God's divine healing light into my mind, body and spirit, creating a state of total well-being.***

WINTER

How to Get Ready for the End Times

Affirmation: *When I stay focused on the present my life is richer and more peaceful.*

According to the Mayan calendar the end of the world was supposed to take place December 21, 2012. (They have a calendar that's 2000 years old and that's the last date on the calendar.) They were an extremely intelligent race, and some have even speculated that they were helped either by visitors from another solar system or another spiritual realm.

Prophets and seers have predicted the end of the world since its beginning. You've probably seen one or two doomsayers standing on a city street corner wearing a placard or shouting the slogan "Repent, the End is Near!" The Apostles, especially Paul, were sure the Second Coming was to take place in the near future. John wrote about his visions of the world's demise in Revelations. Nostradamus, the world-renowned seer from the 1500s, predicted the path of our destruction.[13] Edgar Cayce, the "Sleeping Prophet" from the early 1900s also had some predictions about end times and Jeane Dixon, an American actress and famous astrologer, was pretty sure that she also knew when we would disintegrate. There have been too many willing to tell us when we will destruct.

The "Preppers" are a group of people preparing for Armageddon, the end of the world. They have shelters and stocks of food, water, and

---

[13] There's a special about his predictions that's been aired for years on the History channel that I find be quite unsettling.

weapons. They rotate supplies so that they are always fresh and ready. They say it's a way of life to be ready for the inevitability of the end times. In the 1960s people were preparing just like today. Many built bomb shelters with the same sense of doom that presently exists (I wonder if some of the Preppers are using those same shelters for their storehouses?) When I was a child we used to have air raid practices in which we would have to hunker down under our plastic school desks. I can't imagine how that would have saved us from anything especially from something as destructive as a bomb.

I'm the queen of prevention. Tell me something that might help keep me safe and healthy and I'm all over it. I brush and floss, moisturize, exercise, pray, and meditate. I'm ready! I take my vitamins and keep a bottle of baby aspirin next to the bed and in my travel bag. I'm ready! I go for my yearly physical, dental exam, and mammogram. I'm ready! Give me some guidance about how to stay strong, healthy and safe, and away I go following the rules. One year I signed up for a class that was offered by my town about "disaster preparedness." I wanted to know what needed to be collected, ready for instant departure should a hurricane, tornado, or a tsunami threaten us even if I did't live anywhere near the ocean. One cannot be too careful. Edgar Cayce has predicted that large parts of the United States coast line will fall into the ocean and those of us living inland will have prime beach property. It doesn't matter that it was supposed to happen in 1998. A prophet can get their time lines a little skewed. If the apostle Paul could be off by a few thousand years, Edgar can be forgiven for missing his target date by a few decades.

When we experienced the terrorist attack on September 11, 2001, I know I was not the only one who thought the world was on the brink of destruction. Just like Alan Jackson's song refers to in "Where Were You When the World Stopped Turning?" I found myself in church, holding hands with strangers. I needed the comfort of my faith and my belief system took me to Mass. I periodically attended daily Mass and usually we had about twenty people present. On September 12, 2001, the chapel was full. Father Bill Schmidt said the Mass that day. His sermon was very powerful. He shared that no one knows when the end of the world will take place, no matter what they claim.

I am here, however, to tell you the prophets are right. The world is going to end. Our world as we know it will one day be gone. Certainly, we will all at some time forfeit our personal space on this earth. Each of us will at some time in the future no longer be here. Perhaps too, our earth as we know it will also no longer be here. I've read where plans are being made for the creation of colonies on other planets in case we may need to evacuate. Life as we know it will change.

I do not, however, plan to join the Preppers. I'm not sure how I would react should I be faced with Armageddon and I'm hoping I won't find out, but I don't want to believe I would be someone who would want to survive at the expense of my friends and loved ones. I can't imagine my having food and shelter and denying it to those in need. If I did, who would I be? Not someone I'd want to know or someone of whom I'd be proud. I'm sure that would not be what my Lord would want of me either.

We all leave our mother's wombs reluctantly. We have no desire to leave the warmth and comfort of our known existence for the cold, new world we are destined to enter. For most of us it's so much easier to stay in our comfort zones but just like the child at birth, we are thrust out into the new, into the unknown. Every ending has a beginning. If our global world as we know it does end, what will our new world be like? Perhaps, as many have said, we are on the cusp of a new age. Perhaps, it will be a world that is kinder, gentler, more loving. We too will move on. I believe we will move from this life into another and that, too, will be a place of comfort and peace and love. I decided therefore not to focus on the future and the unknown. That was part of Father Bill's homily on September 12, 2001. He reminded us that our responsibility was to live each day as if it were our last. We get to choose to focus on living life to the fullest each day, each moment. We can choose to focus on our relationships, our gifts and the preciousness of our existence and not to spend our energy futility preparing for the unknown. By choosing to focus on the present, with a rational awareness of the future, we can live lives that are richer and calmer and more compassionate. I'm ready!

> *"Yesterday is gone. Tomorrow has not yet come. We have only today. Let us begin."*
> Mother Teresa

You Can Change the World

Affirmation: *All things are possible through God.*

Forty women were present at the weekend retreat. The command was "Women of God, you are called to change the world." I panicked. Maybe now would be a good time for me to run out of the room. I'm working hard enough trying to be the best me possible or some days I'm working on simply accepting myself just as I am. I really couldn't imagine being responsible for the entire world. I've felt responsible for my entire world for years, my family, friends, and community. It's a daunting exercise and now here I am being told—not asked, but told—I am being called to take on saving the entire world.

Yes, I believe the world needs help. I believe it needs to change. It doesn't take much awareness to know our world is very troubled and sad. I pray daily for wisdom for our world leaders, a prayer introduced to me by a friend of long ago and I pray daily for world peace. Can you imagine how different life would be if we were we all at peace with one another? At the least maybe they'd take away the security lines at the airport and we could leave on our shoes, belts, and watches.

"Let there be peace on earth and let it begin with me. Let there be peace on earth a peace that was meant to be." We sing this song, "The Prayer of Saint Francis," often in church. My dear friend and guide, Valerie Kelly, used to emphasize the need for more feminine energy in the world and how much better off the world would be with a stronger female presence. I would hope that if we have not moved too far away from our feminine selves, women running the world would lead to a kinder, more nurturing place and people. I believe most women are very protective of the greatest product of their lives and would do all in their power to prevent sending their children off to suffer the casualties of war and perhaps to die.

Creating Positive Affirmations, Living an Intentional Life

At the Not So Big Life workshop, Sarah Susanka encouraged us to "run toward those things" of which we are afraid. She suggested some of our greatest learning experiences would come from not retreating from that which repels us. I took a deep breath and decided to continue with the church program for which I had registered. After eight weeks of study, a weekend retreat was being presented and I decided to go all the way and see what other life lessons might come my way.

The number of women who had taken the time and made the effort to attend this event, made me realize how much need there is for women to be spiritually fed and to join forces. I had decided not to worry about the command to "save the world" but instead to allow the richness of the rest of the program's material and the power of the women's spirit to empower and nurture me. Our first speaker was Theresa Davis.

There she stood, a tiny woman perhaps in her late 70s or early 80s, ready to share with us the secret of leading a rich, powerful life. She had been with the lay ministry, Madonna House, for 57 years. As she spoke, I felt the walls around my heart fall. Her manner of sharing did not cause me to erect any protective barriers. I had no resistance to her. I just wanted to absorb all she had to share. It was a very unusual response for me. I must confess to being quite a skeptic, always questioning, but not this morning. This morning when Theresa's time was up, the whole group moaned, "No, let her continue." She, too, was calling us, the women of God, to change the world but not by ourselves, together and by allowing God to work in and through each of us. "Yes," I thought, "all things are possible with God."

Theresa went on to say that we are all being called to become saints. Oh, no! I was just getting my head around "saving the world" and now, I need to also become a saint! Being a cradle Catholic I'm somewhat familiar with many of the saints and I am here to tell you, they did not have an easy time of it. The saints of old were tortured and killed. Many appeared just plain crazy, hearing the voice of God and going off to do really weird stuff. Our most recent saint, Mother Teresa, had a very difficult life. The women and men of her order only possess a few worldly items: a sari, a bucket, and a thin mattress. Certainly she made the world a better place and I am in awe of her and her works, but I like the comforts of home. I like bathing in a tub or shower and not using a bucket, and I really like my bed and my clothes. Sainthood is not something I'd ever had on my radar but Theresa Davis was not going to let me off so easily. Her words and tone had already drawn me to her and now she was going to give me a few tools to help lead me down a holier path. The first tool was being present to "the duty of the moment," so simple, yet so very difficult.

The call of every spiritual discipline I have ever studied or read about is, "Be present to the moment." Live consciously! Theresa shared that, "God is only present in the moment." Then came the second step towards sainthood. She echoed Mother Teresa's famous saying, "Do little things with great love," again, so simple and yet so very difficult. Finally, she extolled us to live more simply. The question was, "What's holding you back? What is the baggage you are lugging around?" I immediately thought this was going in the direction of the sari, bucket, and thin mattress but no, it was way harder than that. Our "baggage," Theresa said, was our anger, resentments, pride, self-deceit, envy, and greed. I immediately wanted to grab that bucket and just go with that. This was way more difficult. Yes, difficult but certainly well worth working toward, and certainly a project in which I'm sure God would like to be involved.

My faith teaches that once we die and enter into heaven we all become saints. I think this is a good thing because while I want to do my part to "save the world" and I'm willing to accept that I'm being called to be a "saint," the probability of my achieving these feats even with God's help seems to me quite slim. On days when I'm simply trying to accept myself as I am, I'll know at least there's great hope for me, for all of us, in the future and in the afterlife.

Field of Dreams

Affirmation: *If I can imagine it, I can achieve it; if I can dream it, I can become it.*

"If you build it, they will come." Do you remember that phrase? It was used in the film *Field of Dreams*, starring Kevin Costner. Costner portrayed a farmer in Iowa who kept seeing the spirits of old baseball players in his corn field. He decided to mow down his crop and build a baseball field for his spiritual visitors. Most people thought he was crazy but he went ahead anyway. At the end of the movie cars are lined up for miles, filled with people hoping to see what Kevin's character was seeing: the late, great baseball players.

Over the years, I've been fascinated by people who decide to build a field of dreams sometimes hoping—sometimes expecting—people to come. One example of this is my fiddle teacher, Mara Shea. She's a marvelous teacher and a wonderful person. At one point she decided to sponsor a fiddle class at our local Senior Center. How many older adults do you think there are who want to learn to play the fiddle? It didn't matter to Mara. The Center told her she needed to have at least four people for the class to happen, and exactly four people signed up. Some weeks only one person showed up, but that didn't matter to Mara; she was always there. At this point, Mara has taught her Thursday morning class for five years and each year more students enroll. In 2013 we were up to six fiddlers. There's little doubt that every year there will be more of us.

The water aerobics class at my mountain community is another example. We "lost" our instructor, so one of our members, Annemarie Halbeck, offered to facilitate the class. She'd never taught before but she'd taken a lot of water classes and it was her main form of exercise. She taught the class every Monday, Wednesday, and Friday morning during the summer months. Initially, there were six of us who came to class, but if no one came, she exercised alone. She did a great job. As of 2013 there were about fifteen people attending on a regular basis. She built the "field" in the water and people were definitely interested.

I know it's true that people may not come to what you think is a good idea even if you're willing to dedicate yourself to it. At one point in our lives, my eldest daughter, Melissa, and I opened a stationery store. We had it for five years. We were there every day except Sunday and we were knowledgeable and very responsive to our customer's needs but during those five years the Internet exploded in popularity. We found we were a great place for people to see and touch the product that interested them, but then they'd go home and buy it online from a large distributor. Sometimes they actually brought it back to us if they weren't satisfied or if they had made a mistake in ordering. There was nothing we could do except encourage them to order it from us. We guaranteed all our work. But the stores on the Internet sold our products for a lower retail price than we could purchase at wholesale. By the time we closed the store we had days when we wondered if we had forgotten to take down the "closed" sign. But if we hadn't tried at all we would have never known if it was a good idea or not and we would have missed out on an experience that for the most part we really enjoyed.

When I decided to have a beach retreat for women breast cancer survivors (PinkRibbonYogaRetreat.org) I wasn't sure anyone would come. I had no idea if anyone else would be interested or if I could find people that would want to help. At our first meeting a dozen people showed up and volunteered to help. Our first year we had brochures and flyers that we distributed anywhere we could. We had about 23 women attend. In our eighth year we merely opened registration up online and we had 35 women (our maximum) register almost immediately. It made me sad

that we had to limit our registration to only 35 women, but just like the fiddle class and the water aerobics, we had built our "field of dreams" and people came.

Do you think that most successes result from only sheer dedication and determination? I often think of Thomas Alva Edison and the fact that it took him 12 years and 5,999 tries to develop the light bulb. How about "Pistol" Pete Maravich, one of the greatest basketball players of all time? He never put the basketball down. He slept with it. He could spin it on his hand for over an hour without stopping. Sister Mary Margaret of the organization "A Place for Women to Gather" had a dream. She was the first in her community, The Sisters of the Holy Cross, to create a place for women to share their insight and knowledge. As of 2012, A Place for Women to Gather had been open for ten years, serving hundreds of women in their quest for personal and spiritual growth.

My husband is one of my heroes. His dedication and determination has led him to professional and personal success beyond that of most people. We often find ourselves looking around at our life and being awed by the blessings we've reaped, blessings that came from hard work and integrity and a close connection with our God. Sandy is now on his third or fourth career. I've lost count. He's become a motivational speaker. He wrote a book called *Humanity at Work; Encouraging Spirit, Achievement and Truth to Flourish in the Workplace*. He then began building his "field." I was fascinated watching him go about creating and pursuing his dream. There is little doubt in my mind that the day will come when people will be lining up to hire him for their inspiration and education. In fact, many people have already discovered him.[14]

I am sure you too can think of many examples of "true dreams." Some may be of famous people, some may be those of friends and family. "If you build it, they will come." What about you? What have you thought about creating? What have you already created? Do you have a dream you're willing to commit to?

> *"If you can imagine it, you can achieve it; if you can dream it, you can become it."*
> William Arthur Ward

---

[14] You can find him at: www.SantoCosta.com

Perfecting Christmas

Affirmation: *I let go of perfection.*

As I write this Christmas is almost upon us. There are only two days left. My entire family will be here: All our children, all our grandchildren, all the in-laws, and both of our mothers. There might even be a few coming of whom I'm not aware. I feel blessed to be surrounded by so many loving people and the really good news is everyone usually likes everyone else. I am also blessed because I have the good health and the energy to do everything I like to do for Christmas.

I love to decorate the house. I would like to leave my Christmas tree up all year long. I love having red sparkly and gold glitzy things all around. It makes me feel warm and enlivened. I love to put together the Christmas cards and I love to "snail mail" them out to all the people on my list. I like recalling the memories associated with each one as I write their names and try to take enough time to say a small blessing over each envelope. I usually send a photo card and I love to go through the year's photos, re-live the memories and choose the best picture of each person. I also like to do a family photo calendar. I was so excited the first time I saw such a thing. I knew it would be something I would try. The first year it took me days to get it done. The good news is now it only takes hours. I'm sure someday I'll be even more efficient but it's OK either way. I love going over the year's photos and putting different memories on each monthly page and then putting my loved one's photos in the date box of their birthday.

In the South Christmas starts the day after Thanksgiving, but it starts much earlier in the stores (earlier and earlier each year, it seems). Some of my neighbors have their houses decorated before Thanksgiving but for many of us in North Carolina the decorations go up Thanksgiving weekend. I love that too. I get to enjoy the festive sprit in my home for about a month.

Even though I am crazy about all the activities involved in our celebration, I can stress out. There is good stress and there is bad stress but stress is stress and it can be exhausting. Most of our traditions seem to be activities that I have taken on as my responsibility. I purchase most of the gifts. I plan the menu. I buy most of the food. I wrap most of the presents. Most women reading this probably have many other items for which they feel responsible. I usually handle most of our activities fairly well unless life happens. You know about life. Life is what happens in between all of our plans.

I like order. I like things neat and clean. There are times when I'm sure my desire for order borders on obsessive-compulsive. The truth is there is only so much time and energy and money and at some point I have to let some things slide. It's a requirement to maintain my mental and physical health. I have several artist friends and they occasionally speak about what happens to their art work when they strive for perfection. They add one more dab of paint, one more stroke of the brush, one more line to the drawing, or one more turn to the potter's wheel and they have ruined their work. From them I have taken the lesson that while I strive to do my best, I cannot always expect perfection from myself. When I do that, I will consistently ruin my work and ruin the enjoyment I take from the process. I must tell myself, ***"I let go of perfection."*** The more I practice releasing myself from unrealistic expectations the more joyful I am. The more I practice letting go of going for the gold the more relaxed I am. When I can be centered and calm, my Christmas, my life and the life of many of those around me is filled with the things that are truly important to me and to the world: peace, love, joy, compassion, and gratitude.

A Year-End Review, Looking Back Before You Go Forward

Affirmation: *I examine the past with an eye on my best future.*

The conversation revolved around how different generations use technology. Adam, my daughter's fiancé at the time, spoke to me about how those over 50 had to learn about social media; how for those in their late 20s and 30s it was simply an extension of the computer skills they learned as children and how those in their teens today have grown up with social media. It's an integral part of their life, like radio or television is to some. He then went on to tell me that my then 15-year-old granddaughter would have a complete photo history of her life not because we have been photographing her since birth, which we have, but because she posts photos and everyday events on the social media sites and has been for several years. She has been carefully schooled by her parents about the dangers of sharing too much information or about sharing inappropriate information (so far, so good). After our discussion, I found myself thinking how nice it would be for me to have a complete record of my life. The older I become the more there is to remember and the more I seemed to have forgotten.

For me recalling the past can sometimes be quite a challenge unless the event is tied to a significant emotional response. I have at least one friend who can remember the names of all her teachers from elementary school through high school. My sister, Gloria Hafner, can recognize people she hasn't seen in years and my husband's ability to remember where we've traveled and what we've done is amazing. On the other hand I really struggle with those skills. I do, however, remember holding my oldest daughter's hand as we walked together to her pre-school. I remember when my youngest crawled into bed with me early in the morning to hug for a while before she went off to school, and I can recall every one of my son's projects, and there have been many I remember well because of the excitement he generated as he took them on.

The television show *Sixty Minutes* has had two separate programs about memory issues. The first was about people who cannot remember faces, not even the faces of their loved ones. They are not ignorant by any means but that part of their brain simply doesn't hold that information. The same program also looked at people who had no directional skills. They were lucky to get out of their own homes. That part of their brain didn't provide that skill. On the second program they interviewed people who could recall every moment of their lives as if they had a file cabinet in their brains and they could access whatever information they needed, whenever they needed it. At the time of the show, there were only about a dozen people known worldwide with this skill. I am pleased to say I do not have either of these issues or skills. My memory is selective and challenging, but I can easily recognize my loved ones and many others and I have a fairly strong sense of direction but whereas I would like to more clearly remember my past, I would not want to carry every one of those memories with me throughout my life. I think that would be overwhelming and exhausting.

It is, however, very important for me to review the past. It's probably why I keep a journal and a little pocket calendar to write the day's past events. For me, it's like looking in the rearview mirror of the car before changing lanes, because then I am aware of what's going on around me. I have found it to be very helpful to put together a yearly family photo calendar. Going back over the year's significant events really helps me to recall that which was important to me and what brought me joy. Otherwise, the year all blends together. Then the years all blend together and those highlights I so enjoyed and those lessons I learned are lost. It's the difference between living a life of many different colors and tastes, and living one that's gray and bland.

I have a monthly and a yearly practice of asking myself ten questions that I feel will improve the quality of my life going forward. I gathered these several years ago from a newspaper article by syndicated columnist Sharon Randall.

1. What was the hardest thing I had to do this year?
2. What was the most fun?
3. What were the milestones?
4. What was my biggest accomplishment?
5. What's something I wanted to do but didn't?
6. What was my biggest surprise?
7. What was the best thing I did for another?
8. What was something I worried about that I don't worry about now?
9. What made me proud?
10. Describe a moment I want to remember.

For me, the moment in 2011 that I most want to remember is when most of my family took a trip to Walt Disney World. On our last evening there the other adults chose to go back to the condo. I chose to hang out with my four grandchildren. We spent the night watching the light shows, the fireworks, and the people. It warms my heart and feeds my soul to remember that evening.

I feel the only reason to review the past, is to find a way to live better in the future. Look it over, learn the lesson and then let it go. The last part may be the hardest lesson of all.

Manifesting the New Year

Affirmation: *I am always manifesting; I manifest to my highest and best.*

The beginning of a new year can be filled with mixed feelings and expectations. Many years ago the comic strip *For Better or For Worse* had a New Year's Day cartoon of Elizabeth, the young daughter, opening her new calendar and exclaiming "I can't wait to put down all the wonderful things that will happen." If I were to closely examine my reaction to a new year it would not necessarily be filled with the expectation of delightful events. I find I must be very aware of the feeling of dread that can present itself as I look forward to the future, especially if I am dealing with post-Christmas letdown. It takes a conscientious effort to turn my thinking around and to prepare myself for the delights that I hope are waiting for me. Every year, I am faced with the choice of "Faith or fear."

I truly believe we manifest our own realities. I am always manifesting and I want to manifest to my highest and best. I don't like to leave the quality of my life to chance. There are always things I can be working on that will enrich my life. One of my practices of many years is to take time at the beginning of the new year and to decide what's important to me and what I'd like to see manifest itself. I do this by looking at the different aspects of my life and seeing what I want to emphasize and concentrate on. I divide my life into several categories. Certainly, you can choose any that might work for you but mine are: Spiritual, Physical, Mental, Family and Friends, Material, Community, and Financial. I set intentions and create affirmations for each section. An intention is a phrase stated in the present tense about something which you want to bring into reality. The affirmation is a phrase or group of sentences clearly articulating the intention. It is also stated in the present tense, as if it's already a reality.

> *Spiritual*: One of my intentions is to meditate daily. My affirmation is, "I meditate once a day for at least 20 minutes." Another Spiritual goal is to increase my faith. My affirmation is, "I pray daily and I attend church weekly. I participate in my Small Christian Community and look for other opportunities to participate in events that will increase my faith."
>
> *Physical*: My intention here is to be of optimal health. What steps do I need to take that will lead to that state? My affirmation is, "I eat 'clean' at least 80 percent of the time. I look for fun ways to exercise, and I do some form of exercise daily."
>
> *Mental*: I know I am either "green and growing" or "ripe and rotten." I read a wonderful news article about a 93-year-old man who recently learned to read and write. He then went on to publish a book. That's my intention: to be learning as long as I'm alive. So my affirmation is, "I look for opportunities that help me grow. I am studying the fiddle and I am open to all learning opportunities: travel, classes, lectures, documentaries, and new people and experiences."
>
> *Family and Friends*: When it comes to this category, I usually focus on what I'd like the most if my family and friends were thinking about me. I would like more of their time and attention. Therefore, my affirmation is, "I carve out a regular time to spend with each of my loved ones and look for opportunities when we can share experiences."

Material: I include this category because we live in a material world and it needs to be addressed. In the past I've focused on living in a different house or perhaps making the house I live in different, lighter, brighter, and more comfortable. This time my affirmation is, "I only keep the things I love and use and let go of the rest."

Community: I believe community is essential to everyone's well-being. My affirmation is, "I volunteer my time, treasure and talent to help those who are within my power to help. I focus my talents on projects that I know make a positive difference in the lives of others. I enjoy sharing my home with my friends and family and look for opportunities to do so."

Financial: This affirmation is, "I attract financial prosperity. I look for opportunities that increase our income and that decrease our expenses."

I have found that there is great power in simply writing out my intentions and creating the affirmations. I like to review last year's at the beginning of the New Year. I am always fascinated by how many of the intentions have come to fruition, how many of the affirmations are now reality, and I'm fascinated and grateful that I took the time to work on manifesting the year ahead. What do you want your New Year to manifest? Take your time, give it some thought and put your intentions on paper. Fill in your calendar now before the year starts. Fill it in with all the things you want it to hold: joy, love, hope, peace, great health, adventure. It's yours; it's waiting for you to claim it and to manifest it.

Finding Your Joy

Affirmation: *I intentionally choose those things that bring me joy.*

My friend Ann Baucom, a wise and gifted woman, once told me January was her favorite time of the year. She loved the opportunity to slow down and stay in because she could look at the long-range view of the months in front of her and plan her life. She was very deliberate about what was important to her and what brought her peace and joy, and she took the cold, dreary month of January to envision all those opportunities that she could create to nurture herself. She presented me with a very different view of the long dark month than I had previously experienced. Certainly, I had used the opportunity of a new year to make plans and to set intentions but I hadn't really embraced sitting with my dreams for the upcoming year and appreciated the month as a time of gestation for those dreams to grow.

I love to rise before the sun. In Clyde Edgerton's novel *Walking Across Egypt*, protagonist Matti Rigsbee rises before dawn and sits outside as the blackness becomes gray and then light. The author describes how this is Matti's favorite time of day. She relishes the new day and awaits the gifts it will bring with it. It's one of my favorite passages. I could feel her peace and joy as she waited for the light of day to seep through the darkness and wash away the night. I once had the opportunity to go to one of Clyde's readings and was delighted to hear him read the very same passage I so loved. That description completely changed my perception of how I perceived the beginning of a perfect day: rise before the sun, make a cup of tea, light a candle (or in the colder months, a fire), sit quietly, pray, write, breathe, and go gently, softly into the day. The way I choose to begin my day flavors the way I live that day. The way I begin my year flavors the way I live that year. It's not very different, a dark morning opening into light of day or a dark month opening into a new year.

If we begin something—a day, a year, a job, a marriage, a project—with a sense of excitement and joyous expectation, does that make a difference in how that something proceeds? In the book *The Joy of Appreciative Living,* Jacqueline Kelm recommends three steps that can be implemented in order to increase one's sense of joy. The first step is to write daily three gratitudes. The second step is to think of one thing every day that will bring you joy, and the third step is to take fifteen minutes, once a week, to imagine your ideal life. The premise of the book is that if you do these exercises for 28 days, your level of happiness will increase and even if you then stop doing the exercises you will maintain a higher level of joy than when you began the process. After beginning the program I was driving home one evening right at sunset and the sky was breathtakingly beautiful. "One gratitude to write tomorrow," I told myself. I would have appreciated it even if I wasn't in the process of increasing my joy, but I wouldn't have made a mental note to remember it. It was the difference between capturing the image and just noticing it in passing. I realized I had begun to look for moments of joy to record and that simple process was making me happier.

Shaun Achor, author of *The Happiness Advantage,* has a short TED video on YouTube about using this process for your job. It was originally sent to a dear friend, Kathy Calabrese, a special-education teacher, by the principal at her school. She told me that looking for three gratitudes each day had the same effect on her as it did on me. Certainly, looking for joy has got to be a better approach to improving the quality of one's life than looking for sadness (or worse). One need not only look forward for joy. You get to choose what you focus on in the past. As part of a healing process one of my chiropractors, Joanne Noel in Chapel Hill, North Carolina, had me "reframe" an upsetting memory that she felt had twisted my body in ways I knew hurt but didn't fully recognize. "Why choose to focus on a painful memory?" she said. "Let's change it, or better yet, delete it like an unwanted, useless email."

Then there's steps two and three from *The Joy of Appreciative Living*. For many years I've kept a small Hallmark calendar in my daily journal. Each morning I've recorded one thing that brought me joy and one thing that I did to help another, but the concept of actually planning a joy was new to me. It reminded me of being on a successful diet. I've read that one step is to write down everything you eat but that an even more powerful step is to plan what you're going to eat. With step two from *The Joy of Appreciative Living* I plan what I'm going to feed my spirit.

I love my life; however, I still have dreams and once again I am reminded of God's bounty and of the truth that I cannot fathom the riches that can be found once we connect to the Divine. Why wouldn't I institute a practice that might raise my level of joy? When I feel positive, joyful, and happy, I carry those emotions out into the world and while some may find them to be disarming, most seem to need and appreciate a smile, a warm greeting and even sometimes, a hug. My ideal life always includes optimal health and I work hard to maintain that state. I eat as well as I know how, I exercise daily, I take my vitamins and I don't smoke or abuse my body. I'm invested in dying healthy but good health and an ideal life require more than care for the body. The body will cease to exist one day no matter how well I care for it. I need to focus on the spirit too. As in past planning in January, I carefully considered what my ideal life would include. I didn't take on any resolutions but carefully crafted ten intentions:

1. Pray Unceasingly
2. Forgive Continually
3. Accept and Give Love Freely
4. Hug Whenever Possible
5. Learn Constantly
6. Dance Often
7. Eat Mindfully
8. Recognize the Shadows

9. Smile Early, Laugh Daily
10. Be Grateful, Always and for All Things

May you too craft some intentions that will bring more light and joy into your life and into the lives of all those you love and the lives of all those your life touches.

Embracing Adventure

Affirmation: *I am a bold adventuress.*

This is a very clear example of creating an affirmation to change the way I want to think. I want to believe with all my heart that I am not afraid of most things, especially an "adventure." There are all types of adventures some we choose and some which are chosen for us. I don't care; I want to embrace every one of them. I want to embrace every aspect of life and I think most of life is that which happens between our plans and usually that requires a sense of adventure. Perhaps being a daring adventurer requires all those skills I've worked on over the years and have in my "tool box"?

It seems to me an adventurer or adventuress needs to be flexible. My husband and I were on our way to a vacation and it required us to fly there. We were meeting our daughter and future son-in-law in the Caribbean. I've come to believe anytime flying is involved, some sort of adventure will present itself and all the survival skills I've been practicing over the years will be needed to finish the journey. On this particular occasion, I was right. It seemed anything that could delay a flight happened, from a malfunctioning de-icer, to a sick passenger, to mechanical difficulties. There we sat, going nowhere. After a three-hour delay, we took off. If there were a miracle, we would make our next flight. There might have been one but we weren't aware of it. We missed the next flight by 20 minutes. All of the flights the next day were full. They could send us through Puerto Rico and then onto our final destination. We'd arrive, hopefully, 12 hours after our original time.

The greatest loss I experienced with cancer was the loss of my intuition. I always trusted I knew, without reason, what was going to happen. I had had many life experiences when I knew ahead of time how things were going to work out even when no one else could see it. When the word "cancer" was first mentioned to me, it didn't register. I had no forewarning. I couldn't imagine what they were talking about. I didn't believe them. I just about attacked the poor physician who first uttered "breast cancer" to me. What did he know? That was ridiculous! I knew he was wrong. He wasn't wrong and there I was going on an adventure I hadn't chosen and of which I'd never even dreamed.

I'd always worked hard to be healthy. I exercised, I gave up smoking, I only drank alcohol periodically, and I really did try to eat healthily. After the cancer treatments were discontinued, I began to look at more modalities I could enlist to stay healthy. I've spoken with many people who go searching for those things that will keep disease at bay. It doesn't have to be cancer. It can be heart disease, diabetes, osteoporosis, high blood pressure. The list is long. Sometimes I hear about ailments that only a tiny portion of the population ever experience and hope that I never have to deal with something so rare but rare or not there's always that tiny—sometimes not so tiny—voice that is questioning what is going on inside my body that I have no knowledge of and over which it appears I have no control. Oh, I'm trying to control it. That's what all those extra measures for staying healthy are all about, vegetarian eating, abstaining from alcohol, exercising every day, taking my vitamins, and having my yearly screenings. It's my attempt to keep illness at bay, to trick myself into believing I have control over what's going on but I don't really, do I? Certainly I can do all within my ability but after that, who really knows?

My husband told me a story about a young man, a professor's assistant, who was so anxious about his health that he had stopped living. After the professor listened to his young friend's concerns, the professor talked about his great-grandfather. His great-grandfather had had all sorts of health ailments, including losing an arm in one of the wars, but he wasn't as concerned with disease and death as he was with living. He had a zest for life and it couldn't be dimmed. He wasn't going to go quietly into the night and if he did, he was going to go with the vast, colorful memories of a life well-lived.

Balance is another skill I've worked on over the years. In yoga, you normally have one or two balance poses you practice in every session. There is a balance between living recklessly and living so small that you might as well already be dead. That's where being an adventurer or adventuress comes in. It's deciding to embrace the experience whatever it is or whenever it presents itself.

As we boarded the second plane to Puerto Rico, a petite blonde woman sat in the window seat next to me. I don't remember how the conversation started, probably with just a nod and a hello, like so many casual meetings. We exchanged a few niceties about where we were going and why. I was on vacation with my family, she was returning to one of her two homes, one in Majorca and one in Antigua. She lived on a ship. It was being restored in English Harbor, Antigua. It was a classic and she invited me to come see it. The name? The Adventuress.

We took one day from the delights of the resort and headed out to see some of the island. We finally reached English Harbor. I guess I wasn't really thinking about how to find her ship, but I thought I'd just ask. There were hundreds of ships in the harbor. After a while and a few questions, a delightful young man offered us a ride in his Zodiac. He thought the ship at the very end of the other side of the harbor might be the one for which we were looking. Off we went. Yes, it was her ship, The Adventuress. No, the owner was nowhere to be found but with the mention of her name we were invited aboard for a short tour. It was stunning and certainly something far removed from my realm of experience. I've not been on a lot of sailing ships. In fact the person who gave us the tour was the "sail master." I didn't even know there was such a title.

I kept thinking about my intention to be grateful for all things at all times. If we hadn't missed our flight, I never would have met the owner of The Adventuress. Once again I was faced with the belief that if I'd just relax, trust and rest in God's infinite care, I'd be so much happier, so much calmer. Perhaps I'd even begin to trust my instinct again. Perhaps I'd be able to see the adventure thrust on me with the onset of breast cancer. Maybe if I could embrace that aspect of the diagnosis, the one that lets me see all of life as an adventure, maybe then I could finally fully claim the intention I've had for so very long, ***"I am a bold adventuress."*** I'm not afraid to fully live life and with that, perhaps, like the old man in the story, I'll go to my death with the vast colorful memories of a well-lived life.

Nurturing Relationships

Affirmation: *My friends bless my life; I accept them as they are and treasure their relationships with me.*

I like people. When I've taken the Myers-Briggs personality test, I come out evenly between the introvert and the extrovert. The test doesn't tell you how well you relate to people, but whether or not you get energy from being with people or being alone. The goal is to find a middle ground. For me, I need some of both, and the challenge can be finding that balance.

I remember when I was in graduate school getting my master in social work degree (MSW). My very first course was taught by a dynamite young woman; she was so energetic and knowledgeable, and it was a fun and interesting course. She came in one day and it was immediately noticeable to me that she was not her usual self. As the three-hour class progressed, she seemed to be feeling better. Her energy level seemed to be rising and she seemed to be enjoying the process more and more. When the class ended, I took the time to chat with her and I asked her how she was feeling. She told me she felt great but that when she had first arrived for the class, she had a migraine headache. Teaching the class had helped her eliminate the headache.

I, too, am a migraine sufferer. I've had a few doozies. I can tell you, standing in front of a classroom for three hours and teaching would not be the way for me to eradicate a headache. I need medication and a dark, quiet room. I decided there and then, this woman was getting her energy in a very different way than I was. She was probably a high-level extrovert.

I work very hard at staying connected to my family and friends. I know how important it is for my psychological and physical well-being. It's easier sometimes than others. I seem to be able to putter around the house forever. I love a day when I have nothing scheduled and I get to go about town doing my errands and perhaps stopping somewhere fun for a quiet lunch and an opportunity to people watch.

Sometimes I fall into the trap of finding fault with my family and my friends but how does that improve the quality of my life? If I'm finding fault with them, what are they thinking about me, if they're thinking anything at all? I want to simply enjoy my relationships, even those casual ones that come from interacting with people who are working to help me with all my different projects and errands. I want to like and to appreciate everyone. I know that isn't feasible but I can make an effort.

When I heard a story about the funeral of an elderly woman who had kept a Prayer Pouch, I was intrigued. She had only lived in her new community a short while but was very involved in the lives of all those with whom she interacted. When people shared a concern, she would write it out and put it in her Prayer Pouch. She then made an effort to reconnect with the person to see how they were doing. Her funeral, I was told, had people from every phase of her life; they were from the grocery store, the deli, the church, and the restaurants she frequented. She was described to me as a saint because of her positive effect on the world. She was a missionary in her own part of the world. She cared and so people cared about her.

Relationships can be a tricky thing. I think most of our problems and issues relate to our relationships. There have certainly been a million books about them and how to improve them or deal with them, or understand them. Some of the most famous television shows revolved around relationships: *Seinfeld, All in the Family, Everybody Loves Raymond*, and my favorite, *The Golden Girls*. How are you in your relationships? Are you more at ease with strangers, or in your family circle?

At the time of this entry, I'd been married a long time, 44 years. Every so often, my husband, Sandy, speaks about his "good friend" and then he gives me a name. I cannot tell you how many times I have not had a clue whom the person is that he has mentioned. One day, I asked him why he thought of so many people as being his "good friend." He told me that he chose to think of them that way. He chose to think about and refer to many of his acquaintances as good friends. Sandy is an unusual man in many ways but one quality he has, which I have been told by friends that their husbands do not have, is that he has a huge range of friends and he does a remarkable job of keeping in touch with most of them. I loved the idea that he also claimed all of them as his good friends. Why not? How we think about others is very often how they think about us. I believe it must be very unusual to have someone in our lives that we dislike who likes us.

I've had my struggles. I try hard to get along with everyone but I find some to be easier than others, particularly one person who refers to herself as a "low maintenance" friend. It's the truth, isn't it? Some people we simply flow along with, while others are often trying to pull us upstream. In *Conversations with God*, author Neale Donald Walsch talks about "affability." He says it's not a trait most pay attention to but when it's missing, it's always noticeable. It's defined as the ability to be kind, pleasant, and gracious. I have found one way to appreciate people is to simply accept them for the way they are, not to judge. I value the people in my life and along with valuing them, offer up prayers for their well being and for that of their loved ones. If I choose to believe my friends bless my life, they will. If I choose to believe they are draining my energy and causing me angst, that too will be true. Once again, it depends on the way I choose to think. I want to be affable to all the people in my life and I hope they will respond in kind.

Living a Compassionate Life

Affirmation: *I live a Christ-centered life of love, peace, hope, gratitude and compassion.*

One of the most compassionate people I know is my mother-in-law, Yolanda. She's always been one of my heroines and an amazing role model. As of this writing, I've known her for over 45 years and have never heard her criticize anyone.

Compassion can be defined as "co-suffering," but that's a limited description. For one to be truly compassionate you must try to do something to alleviate another's suffering.

One night Yolanda and I were watching the television show *The Amazing Race*. I was visiting her to help her prepare for her move to Savannah. She had lived in the same house for over 56 years and now, at the age of 90, she was moving to an independent living facility in Georgia. This was her choice.[15] This episode of *The Amazing Race* had a young unmarried couple who were racing from country to country. They were doing fairly well and were leading the race when this episode began. When the episode ended, they were in last place. They lost because one of the challenges was to go down a huge water slide through some sharks and into a pool. The young woman of the team was terrified of heights and sharks. With two of her greatest fears combined, she chose not to finish the race. I was amazed and felt very impatient. "For heaven's sake," I thought, "just get on the slide and get it over with!" Really, it would have been over in two minutes. And then there was Yolanda: "Oh, the poor thing! What are they doing? Why don't they just let her walk down? I can't stand to see her suffering so much." I think if Yolanda had been there, she would have jumped on that slide and gone down it in

---

[15] I keep hoping that when and if I'm 90 I'll get to choose some adventure on which I want to embark and not have the adventure chosen for me.

place of the young woman, even though she, too, is afraid of water. Me? I'm sad to tell you I would have suggested to her partner to just pick her up, put her on his lap and go for it. It really was a wonderful lesson for me to sit there and share this experience with my mother-in-law. I don't think I would have seen it any differently if I hadn't been exposed to her point of view. Then, the final lesson came when the emcee interviewed them and asked her boyfriend how he felt about the whole episode. I thought, "Here it comes! He's going to be so angry!" Instead, he was as compassionate about it as Yolanda had been.

Al-Anon teaches that it's essential to learn to take care of yourself. It's not an easy concept, especially for someone who has been caring for a loved one with an addiction. A lot of the time, many people who attend Al-Anon are enablers. One of their chief skills is taking care of others, sometimes with total disregard for themselves. In the Al-Anon book *The Courage to Change, One Day at a Time,* one of the readings tells a story about a woman who had recently become an Al-Anon member. Every night when she went to bed, she found her drunken husband fallen out of bed and lying on the floor. She'd help him back in bed, cover him up and then finally get to go to bed too. After her first Al-Anon session, she decided she'd in order to better care for herself she'd just step over him and go straight to bed. When she shared her new approach at a meeting, they gently told her she had gone to the other extreme. The next night she used a different approach. She gently placed a blanket on him, then stepped over him and went to bed. She managed to find a place where she could be both compassionate and take care of herself.

My friend works out with a trainer. I knew this personal trainer when he was having terrible back pain and when I saw him again, I asked him how his back was doing. He said it was fine. Then he told me he was pleased he'd had the bad back experience because it made him a better trainer. It made him more compassionate.

I know many people take tragic experiences and use them to better the lives of others. There is story after story of people who chose to use their tragedy as a stepping stone not only for their own recovery but for anyone else who is looking for help with the same type of situation. I am sure it wouldn't take much for you to recall some of the more well known examples. How about the Amber Alert organization? It's an organization begun to help find missing children. I regularly see the signs for missing children on the freeways.

Twenty-five years ago Rachel and Saul Schanberg lost their young daughter Linda to cancer. Before Linda died she asked her mother to make a difference in the Duke Cancer Center. She asked her mom to help people feel cared about and not just cared for. Rachel began the Duke Cancer Patient Support Program (DCPSP) with herself and four volunteers in an office the size of a closet. Today her efforts have created a program world renowned for its care of cancer patients and their loved ones. It's all free. Most hospitals wouldn't consider supporting a program that doesn't bring in any revenue, but because of Rachel's passion and compassion, DCPSP has over 300 volunteers and the most amazing services you can imagine. The impact the program has made on the Duke Cancer Center can be seen in the Center's warm, inviting atmosphere.

Our challenging life experiences offer us two choices: We can become more caring, gentle, and compassionate, or we can become bitter, hard, and reclusive. My intention to be a more compassionate person, to be more Yolanda-like, is a quality I always want to be developing. The main lesson in the book *Coping with Your Difficult Older Parent* (by Grace Lebow) encourages the reader, as caretaker, to try to see life from the parent's viewpoint. When the author rephrased some of the concerns of the parent, using language based on her years of experience, it brought me a greater understanding of the things my parent might have concerns about. I felt a deeper sense of compassion.

I am an ardent believer in the power of prayer. I don't know how it works but I believe it does. I keep a list in the front of my journal of all the people for whom I am currently praying. I always add "especially for those who most need Your mercy." Since practicing compassion requires one to "do" something along with experiencing feelings of empathy, I can pray. If there is no other way for me to bring help and solace to those I am concerned about, it gives me great comfort to know I can offer them up in prayer and to believe that God is blessing them in ways beyond my comprehension. Truly, that's how I want to see myself; that's the person I want to be. If when I die my obituary refers to me as compassionate, I will rest with the satisfaction of a life well lived.

Not If When

Affirmation: *I know life presents many challenges and I have a tool box filled with lots of helpful equipment.*

The conversation was about the chaotic state of my home because of a renovation. Oh, I fully recognized the blessing of being able to perform a renovation but the project had now been going on for months and was running much longer than had been estimated.

I was tired. Way too much energy was being expended on this, not to mention money and I wanted to put my home back in order. The homeowner I was speaking with had just completed building a house, not on her own but she was responsible for all of the decisions and it was a beautiful home, the most stunning home I could ever remember being in. She explained to me that one shouldn't be asking themselves about the "ifs" one might experience during the building process but one should recognize that there would be "whens" and the real question was how was one going to deal with them? What did one need to do to be prepared when issues would come along?

I am an optimist by choice. When someone tells me something is going to go well and work out, I choose to believe them. It's not always the truth. Stuff still happens but I haven't focused on what might go wrong. I am that person who creates positive affirmations. I am that person who expects things to go right.

The Buddhists say one should imagine the glass broken. The Christians refer to the "practice of faith" and the yogi studies a Klesha called *raga* which refers to an attachment to pleasure. Whatever faith you look at they all have one very important feature in common; they recognize that life is not a bowl of cherries. Life has pits and we should be aware of that teaching.

The question that arises is how does one prepare oneself for the difficulties life will present? Certainly going around waiting for the next shoe to drop or for the clouds to appear is not a very joyful way to live one's life but we all know stuff will come along, little things and difficult things with which we will have to deal.

I am someone who is all about maintenance. I was a great Girl Scout. I try to always be prepared. If there is some step I can take to hopefully make life easier or smoother, I will usually take it. I am that person who gets her flu shot every year. I take my vitamins, especially that calcium and fish oil and now extra vitamin D. I brush and floss my teeth twice a day. God forbid they should rot away and fall out. I exercise daily to keep everything in good working order and to hopefully avoid becoming immobile and decrepit. I am the person who buys travel insurance. I'm not worried about any of these things. I just feel like if I can take steps to insure my life goes along smoothly, I should. I have many friends who do not think like me. I have one friend who has never gotten a flu shot and as of this writing, has never gotten the flu. Thank heavens! I also have a friend who never does any maintenance on her home. I am always looking around my house and trying to spiff it up before something drastic happens, like an exploding hot water heater or an ant infestation or, well you can probably add your own stuff to that list.

I have a huge red tool box. I mean I need all those different type of screw drivers just in case the screw is a Phillips or a Flat-head or it's big or very tiny. I know many of you completely understand but my friend, she never does anything to her home until it becomes some sort of an issue for her. She cannot for the life of her understand why I am always doing my best to forestall something in the home from becoming a major investment. I believe that if I take care of it now, it'll be a little problem rather than a huge one. "A stitch in time saves nine." We just don't agree but that's ok. We love one another anyway. Unfortunately, the results of my maintenance approach to life really doesn't seem to make my life that much easier than her life is for her. Things I never even dreamed would occur, occur. The question is, "How can I best prepare for the whens of life? What tools do I have in life's tool box for when a screw comes loose or falls out and everything it's been holding together, falls apart?"

Pray, it's my first defense. I believe in answered prayer. I don't understand how it works but I fully trust that it does.

Journal, I write. It centers me and helps me see things more clearly. It makes me calmer.

Exercise, it is known to increase endorphins and reduce stress. It doesn't matter if you go to your mat to do yoga or take a walk or go play golf. It takes you out of your routine and helps calm you.

Talk to a friend or find a counselor. Pick up the phone or go visit a friend. Don't try to go it alone. Most people like to be helpful and most of us need help to get through life's challenges, sometimes even the little ones.

Watch something funny, laugh.

Give or get a hug or two and finally, remember to *Breathe*. Take a few deep breaths every so often and don't hesitate to sigh them out. Even if you haven't fixed the entire problem with that deep breath, you've at least released it for that moment and life really is about living one moment at a time.

Love Is Your Only Job

Affirmation: *"Remember, your only job is to love."*

There are many poses (*asanas*) in yoga that are designed to help one open the heart space. For example, any sort of back bend will put you in a position where your chest is raised towards the sky, even a slight back bend like Fish pose (*matsyasana*). In her memoir *Eat Pray Love*, Elizabeth Gilbert tells a story about a man she met in the ashram in India who reveals that he'd been seeking an open heart. And then one day he had a heart attack and his heart was literally opened. One need not have surgery to create a more open heart. There are many more gentle ways to accomplish this worthwhile trait.

Many years ago when my children were younger, I found myself struggling with one particular incident. I felt very hurt by this episode and was sharing it with a good friend, Ellen Darst. It really wasn't such a big deal looking back on it but at the time I was upset and I felt I was justified in my complaining. So, there I was moaning about the situation. She listened and then gave me some of the best advice I have ever had in my whole life. She said, "Remember, Jean, your only job is to love."

As a journaler who has written three pages every morning for over 20 years, I have many journals boxed up. Every time I begin a new journal I transfer a few things to the front paper pockets and the beginning pages. I transfer my intentions for the year, my daily prayers, my list of people I am presently praying for, and my positive affirmations. I also write on the inside of the front cover, "Remember, Jean, your only job is to love."

I believe that with all my heart. It's the main message Jesus Christ came to give us. When he was asked "[Jesus], which is the great commandment in the law?" He said to them, "'You shall love the Lord your God with all your heart, and with all your soul, and with all your mind. This is the great and first commandment. And a second is like it, You shall love your neighbor as yourself. On these two commandments depend all the law and the prophets" (Matthew 22:36).

Why do some people seem to have a greater capacity to love than others? Do you think it's because of their DNA or is it because of their upbringing? Is it "nature" or "nurture"? It's probably like most of our traits, a combination of both. But we can learn to love more, love greater. Can we be people who can love no matter what? You've heard the stories about people who forgive their worst enemies. Can we learn to love an enemy? Can we learn to separate the sinner from the sin?

I've been very lucky in my life. I married a man who has a huge heart. I believe he was genetically predisposed to being a loving, kind man and he had the additional advantage of having amazing parents, especially his mother, Yolanda who showed him by example exactly what unconditional love is. I have never heard my mother-in-law say anything that was derogatory about another human being, especially about someone in her family. My husband teases that if we had a bank robber in the family his mom would say, "He's the best bank robber ever!"

On my travels through Ecuador, I was kissed more times in three weeks than I have been kissed in three years. Almost everyone I met gave me a kiss on the cheek and a warm hug. One day we went to the soccer practice of my *consuegra*'s* granddaughter. Six of us sat in the bleachers watching her practice: her three grandparents, her aunt, my son and I. When the girls were finished practicing the entire team came up to the stands to greet us. I watched these teenage girls start down the row kissing and greeting all the grandparents, then they kissed the aunt. I thought they'd stop at that point and was amazed when they continued on to kiss my son and then me, two people they "didn't know from Adam."

*Word to describe the mother-in-law of one's son or daughter.

I know it was a cultural response to greet us all in that manner but at this point in my travels I'd been greeted like this for several weeks. Greeted and welcomed into people's homes, lives and in some cases into their hopes and dreams. As far as I could see these people in this culture responded with more affection and respect than I normally experienced. I had the honor of being hosted by my *consuegra* and I can share with you that the hugs and warm daily greetings and goodnights were freely shared with anyone who happened to be in her home.

When I first received the directive to love no matter what, I remember thinking, "I can do that." I must admit, however, it is easier said than done. There are many in my life that I find very easy to love and there are some I struggle to love. Some days I feel like my heart is closed and hard.

When I am aware of that state I engage my breath to help me open up. I take several deep breaths and visualize my heart expanding in my chest, like a red balloon. I've also done many other "open heart" meditations. These meditations usually involve inviting loving thoughts and feelings into one's heart. First, invite those whom you find easy to love; then invite someone you may be struggling with; and finally, invite yourself. Take the time to allow each person to rest within the warmth of your bosom and then release them and yourself out into the universe, full of light and warmth and wonderful energy, a release that blesses you, them, and the world.

I believe we can learn to love more fully, more deeply, unconditionally. But I think there's a secret and I don't think it's that we need to be born into a family of warm-blooded Latinos or Italians. It's nice if we're born into a loving, affectionate family. It probably makes it easier but the secret is to learn to accept love, to believe you are worthy of love, to believe that you are truly loved, loved for who you are because you are and not for any other reason. We need to believe we are loved first and foremost by God. We need to know without a doubt that we are amazing wonderful beings who deserve to be loved. Once we can fully embrace that concept, we can open our heart to receive and then to give that which we have received. If we don't accept it, we can't; it is impossible to give it out. It's like filling up the car with gas. If you don't open the gas cap and let the gas flow in you won't be able to go anywhere. You'll be stuck in one place, empty and dried out.

What if you approached everyone in life with the thought, "Remember, (your name), your only job is to love?" What kind of an effect would that have on your relationships, on you and on your life? What kind of an effect would that have on our world?

The Fragile Ego

Affirmation: *I maintain a childlike ego.*

The yoga teacher took us from Warrior II into Side Angle. The pose requires you to bend your front leg and lean over it and rest your forearm on your thigh. Normally, your palm is faced downward. "Turn your palm up," she said, "pretend you are holding something fragile, perhaps your ego." I laughed out loud. This is why I practice yoga. I look everywhere for those messages that will enrich my life. I search every day for those insights that will enable me to know myself better so that I may live a fuller, more meaningful existence. This day, it came to me from my teacher, Karin Johnson, at Rex Wellness here in Cary, NC. How fragile is my ego?

One day while attending a class, we were encouraged to go into an asana known as Crow. In this pose you squat down with your feet and knees wide and your palms between your legs, flat on the ground. You are then supposed to raise up onto your palms while balancing your thighs against your upper arms. I've done this pose. It's not easy and requires upper body strength as well as balance. Another reason I practice yoga is to take me out of my comfort zone. When I attempt a pose that I know does not come easily, it makes me feel brave. It's brave with a small "b" but it empowers me when I'm out in the world to be brave, sometimes even "Brave." I took the position and slowly raised up onto my palms and then fell straight over onto my nose. I fell with a very loud "whack!" This particular yoga class had about thirty people in it and I know everyone of them heard the sound of my flop. I hoped they were so involved in trying their own pose that they didn't look up but I was sure everyone was looking at me, if just to make sure I was still alive.

"Yoga is not a competitive sport." I start most of my classes with that statement. "Bring you attention to your mat, into your body." The purpose of yoga is to unite the mind and the body. I usually add, "and the spirit." I believe when we only focus on the physical aspect of the practice we deny ourselves the real essence of yoga. When we practice we are called to be present, to stay in the moment. That's the reason the ancient yogis initially came up with all these contortions. It's almost impossible to stand on one leg with your hands high in the air, Tree pose, and to be thinking about anything other than what you are doing in that moment. You are fully present. It's a gift. It's the main lesson of the practice, stay in the here and the now. Once you learn to do that on your mat, it too is something you can take out into the world and practice in your everyday life.

I was lucky and my fall didn't result in a broken or bloody nose but it did result in a dented ego. Most of the class knows I am a Registered Yoga Teacher and I pride myself on my ability to do some of the more advanced positions and there was my lesson. I was prideful. I am always telling people, "Anyone can do yoga." The response I usually get is that they are not flexible enough. What they are really saying is unless I'm already good at something, I am not willing to try it. Our egos have become the wall that keeps us imprisoned in our small comfortable space. Whenever I think of that fall while attempting the Crow pose I laugh. It was a wonderful lesson. It was humbling and it was exactly what I needed to learn from that day's practice.

In 2012, I attended the NC Senior Follies. One of my fiddle buddies, Constance Belton, was the teacher and choreographer of the line dancing team, The Cary Cure Alls. She and six other women did a mock strip tease to the song Fever. They came out in scrubs and white coats with caps on their heads, surgical gloves and wearing stethoscopes and began to remove one item at a time while they tap danced. (Look them up on YouTube.) They won one of the Gold Medals and were the overall champions. There were about a dozen different acts. Some of the seniors sang, some played musical instruments and one group call themselves The Shakers. They were the Senior Game cheerleaders. The event was pure fun.

After being told to "hold my fragile ego gently in my palm." I began to think of all those other times when my ego prevented me from fully experiencing life. I wondered when did that begin? Certainly as a child I wasn't afraid to try new things. If that were true, one would never learn to walk or to talk. One would never learn anything! Those amazing seniors had put away their egos in order to go onto the stage and share their skills. That's another secret to a full, rich, fun filled life; hold your ego gently and don't let it prevent you from trying something new, something at which you might not be good, something at which you might be terrible but who cares! Life is too short not to experience it all. Gently place your ego down and live life like a child whose is first exploring their world.

The story I heard was about an older successful executive who was with a group of people when the topic turned to, "What have you always wanted to do that you haven't yet done." He told the group he always wanted to try tap dancing. That evening he looked up dance studios in his area and the next day he began his lessons. He loved it! For all I know, he's out there somewhere competing in his local Senior Follies. So maybe I'll try standing on my head in my next yoga class. Maybe!

Epilogue

Dear Friend,

Thank you for sharing this journey with me. I hope these affirmations and stories have both nurtured and embowered you. I hope they have caused you to reflect on your life and how you want to shape it. I begin each of my journal entries with the following prayer. As with this whole book, I share it here with you in case it will serve you but it's even more powerful, just like the affirmations, if you create a prayer of your own.

Loving Jesus,

I invite you to share this peaceful, nurturing, insightful time with me. Time to just be, centering time, creative time. Time to love and to count my blessings. Time to see more clearly my gifts and the gifts held and bestowed by others. Time to shine light on my shadows and to ask and receive forgiveness. Time for joy and for sadness, my lifetime here on these pages.

Lord, be united with me this day and always. I invite you and all those who nurture and guide me, seen and unseen to aid me in bringing glory and honor and praise to this gift of life You have so generously given me.

You know my soul. You know all that is within. Fill me with pure love of You.

Loving Lord Jesus, Blessed Mother, all my Angels and guides be with me all my days in every moment. I invite you to join me and to share in the glory of this life. Amen

Acknowledgements

I am married to a remarkable man as you may have gathered from these stories. Sandy and I have created a wonderful, love filled life and family. It's the greatest gift God has bestowed upon me, that of allowing me to share this life with this amazing man and to also share it with my children: Melissa, Joey, and Ellen, their spouses: Larry, Belen, and Adam, my grandchildren: Isabelle, Owen, Joe, and Sam and my other family members and dear, dear friends.

Thank you also goes to:

My good friend, Pam Burnette, who encouraged me from the beginning. Her loyal following of Creating Positive Affirmations and her positive evaluation of each one has kept me steadily moving forward to create this compilation.

My amazing study group, the Seekers: Joanne Dawe, Jean Scholz, Joanne Dryer, Travis Tracy and Rita Bahn. Our journey together both as younger women and into the later part of our lives has brought me insight, joy, excitement and has gifted me with an ongoing attitude of adventure about the future.

Sindy Martin who has helped me publish my blog and has lifted me up with each entry affirming the power of my intentions.

All those readers who have taken the time to comment either in person or on Facebook. It's been such a joy to accidentally meet someone and have them tell me they've been reading Creating Positive Affirmations and that the writings have made a positive impact on their lives.

Thanks to Oie Osterkamp for his generous introduction and his constant affirmations about completing this project.

CPSIA information can be obtained
at www.ICGtesting.com
Printed in the USA
FSHW021812061220
76498FS